D0527570

Dog training

Dog training

All the ideas and techniques
you need to transform your dog into
a well-behaved, sociable companion

Stella Smyth and Sally Bergh-Roose

To all those dogs we've loved and lost who taught us so much.

First published in 2005 by
Collins, an imprint of
HarperCollins*Publishers*
77-85 Fulham Palace Road
Hammersmith, London W6 8JB

The Collins website address is:
www.collins.co.uk

Collins is a registered trademark of HarperCollins Publishers Limited.

09 08 07 06 05
6   5   4   3   2   1

A catalogue record for this book is available from the British Library

This book was created by Kinsey & Harrison for HarperCollins*Publishers* Limited

Project Editor: James Harrison
Designer: Edward Kinsey
Editor: Louisa Somerville
Photographer: Tracy Morgan Animal Photography
Cover design: Cook Design
Front cover photograph: © Photonica/Masahiko Taira

ISBN 0 00 719980 5

Some of this material previously published by Collins as: *Dog Training Handbook*, 2001

Colour reproduction by Colourscan, Singapore
Printed and bound by Printing Express Ltd, Hong Kong

Authors' note: Dogs obviously come in both sexes, but to simplify our training message we have used 'he' rather than 'he/she' or 'it' when referring to any dog.

contents

Introduction

This book is intended to be a beginner's guide to training your dog step by step. We feel it is a shame that so many people get a dog or puppy and only later, when a problem occurs, do they worry about training.

Tried and tested training

In this book we aim to show our training techniques, which we have refined over years of practice, to help owners achieve a smoother handling of their dogs. The training methods illustrated have been used with our own dogs, which have gone on to do competition work and been happy family pets.

Between us over the past 25 years or so we have had a selection of dogs, from working sheepdogs to German Shepherds, Labradors and Australian Cattle Dogs. They have joined us at varying ages – some were carefully selected as puppies, others were older dogs who came into our lives by chance – but all of them have been loved dearly and all responded very successfully to the simple training methods we present here.

Learning to train is like learning to drive

Our training techniques may appear at first glance to be very regimented, a bit like when you are learning to drive. We are instructed to be very precise, sitting up just so and holding our hands on the wheel at exact positions. Thinking all the time about how and what we are doing. At first we are very ham-fisted, trying to think and act all at the same time.

Eventually it comes more naturally and hopefully we will pass our driving test, then we relax a bit. We may not be quite so precise with our actions and position, but we should be safe, reliable drivers. If you use the same degree of precision while teaching your dog, he should find it easier to understand and learn what you are trying to teach him. If you are consistent and precise in your actions, your dog will know what he has to do in response. In time it will become second nature to you both and while you may not be so precise your dog will carry out your requests with a high degree of reliability.

Training is a two-way street
Never get away from the fact that owning a dog should be an enjoyable experience, for you, your family and the dog. Training is not only for control of the dog but also for communication with the dog. A dog that is well-trained leads a much fuller life. As he is not a problem he is more likely to be taken everywhere as a member of the family. The more the dog is exposed to the world in general the more well-rounded his attitude will become, and he will learn from all his experiences. Once the lines of communication have been opened it becomes easier to teach more exercises. Certainly the first steps are always the slowest and hardest to master, but once achieved, they can be built on depending on how much (or how little) energy and enthusiasm you can muster to continue the training.

There are many qualities you need for successful dog training: patience, timing, commitment, enthusiasm and understanding, to name but a few. But the greatest asset is a sense of humour: knowing that sooner or later your dog will make a fool of you – and being able to laugh when it happens.

Size does matter

The size of the dog frequently has a bearing on its owners' attitudes to training. Small dogs are generally considered to be much less of a problem, whether they be adult or puppy, because they can be unceremoniously picked up at the first hint of trouble. This does not solve any problems, it just changes them. Many owners of small dogs tend to tolerate their dog's bad behaviour, possibly because they still think of them as puppies because of their size. Puppies of large and giant breeds tend to have the opposite problem. They become very large at a young age and because of their size their owners often expect too much of them – yet mentally they are still babies.

Owner's responsibilities

Anyone who owns a dog has a responsibility to the dog, themselves and society in general, to care for it to the best of their ability. For example, it is a requirement to have your dog identifiable and that may mean just a collar and tag, or a microchip or tattoo. Another serious consideration should be veterinary health insurance. What will happen if the dog becomes ill or has an accident? Can you afford an operation that may cost hundreds or thousands of pounds? Veterinary health insurance is expensive but may be a godsend at a distressing time when your pet is ill. At least you won't have to worry about the cost of treatment...

The owner's responsibilities also include preventing the dog from being a nuisance. Training is critical. Being firm does not mean that your dog will not love you. In fact the opposite is the case: terrible mental suffering can be caused to the dog who has no clear ground rules. The potential for the increase in mutual love and respect that can be developed during training is enormous. If this book helps you to appreciate that fact, then it will all have been worthwhile.

When to start training?

Many people wait until their new dog is six months old before seriously thinking about doing some form of training, as historically this was considered the norm. These days we are a lot more enlightened and realize the vast benefits of socializing puppies and channelling their behaviour at an early age.

Veterinary advice tends to suggest not taking your puppy outside before it has been vaccinated. However, this may mean the puppy is missing out on crucial experiences which he needs to develop into a stable adult. Obviously it may not be advisable to take him to the local public park and risk him meeting dogs whose health status may be in question. Nor would you be advised to let him sniff around all the lamp posts and trees that have been scent marked by passing dogs.

However, he should be taken out to see and meet as many new things as possible, certainly everything he will need to cope with in his new life. For example, get him used to travelling with you in the car, with a new experience at the end of the trip, even if it's only, say, to visit a friend's house for a titbit. You may not consider this to be training but under your guidance your new dog is learning all the time.

Praise and reward

This book is designed to be a hands-on manual which can be of benefit to owners of dogs of any age or breed. One of the problems we have found over many years in our training classes is the clumsy and awkward way in which owners handle their dogs, especially when the dog is on the lead. Far too often the dogs are pushed and pulled around and given a multitude of conflicting signals that bear no relation to the owner's verbal requests. This leads to frustration for the owner and total confusion for the dog. Our training methods are based on being kind to the dog, with the emphasis on praise and reward. Follow our course and you will find these methods do work.

owning

a dog

'A dog is for life, not just for Christmas'. The message still does not seem to get through to many people before they buy a dog, as the large numbers in rescue homes suggest. A dog is a commitment 24 hours a day, seven days a week.

Home alone

Bad habits quickly creep in and hinder good training if you don't plan ahead. Try to establish a routine with your new dog and stick to it. Have you thought through what will happen when you aren't at home? Neglect can spoil all your hard work.

Whatever the weather

So what are you going to do when you wake up one morning to find the weather is foul? Taking the dog for a walk on a nice sunny day is very pleasant. However, he still needs a walk, day in and day out even if it is raining, windy and freezing cold. Are you prepared for the times when he comes indoors in winter, covered in mud and willing to share it with you and the furniture?

▼ Dogs left at home for long periods of time will tend to find their own amusement. Lots of noisy barking at passers-by, as well as chewing, are two favourite pastimes.

◀ Be forewarned that having a dog does not come cheap. A huge variety of foods as well as a vast array of equipment and toys for dogs are available at specialist outlets. These stores can also be useful sources of canine information and advice.

Weighing up your dog's welfare

Have you thought about what the dog does for the rest of the day after his walk? The novelty may wear off for the kids, and then what? Even if their initial enthusiasm remains, you, as the adult, are ultimately responsible for the dog's welfare. Even a guard dog needs other things to do than just guarding the house. Any dog left alone can get bored and destructive. Young dogs in particular may get into mischief if they have the run of the house and are left unsupervised. A lot of damage can be caused in a short time by enthusiastic claws and jaws! And there will be hair shed indiscriminately, especially when your dog is moulting. Have you factored in the extra housework?

And don't forget the costs – the minimum equipment needed will include a bed, lead, collar, grooming brush or comb, and food and water bowls. Assuming your dog is fit and healthy, he will still need an annual visit to the vet for vaccinations and a health check. He will need worming on a regular basis, and possibly flea treatment for himself – the cleanest dog can pick up the occasional unwanted 'pet' – and the home.

The importance of building a relationship

Are you willing to find the time to make the effort to build a relationship with your dog? It doesn't just happen. Like all relationships, it needs to be worked at to develop fully. The best-behaved dog usually has an owner-trainer who has established a bond between them. They truly enjoy each other's company, are relaxed together, and the dog is socially acceptable. So if you now appreciate the responsibilities of owning a dog, and you still want to go ahead, at least we have forewarned you!

Which breed?

**Now that you are definitely going to get a dog it is worth
remembering that while all breeds are capable of learning
training exercises, it is wise to consider the characteristics
of different breeds before you start. And bear in mind that
small breeds mature more quickly, both physically and
mentally, than large breeds.**

Making your choice

You stand a better chance of your dog fitting
into your lifestyle if you have given some
thought to size and coat type, not to mention
his genetic background. If you want a lapdog,
don't assume a Jack Russell Terrier will be
a good choice. He may be small but he was
bred to work, so he may not want to be
a couch potato. The beautiful Afghan Hound
may be large and energetic but have you time
for his coat care as well?

Years of selective breeding have given us a
huge variety of dog breeds to choose from but
most were bred with a specific purpose in mind.
It is worth doing some research to learn a little
about the breeds before making your selection.

Classification

All breeds are classified into groups, roughly
based on the purpose for which they were
originally developed. This can have a bearing on
the difficulties you may encounter in training
your dog. Scent hounds were bred to follow
their noses – ask any Beagle or Basset Hound
owner how deaf their dogs can be when
they're on the trail of an interesting smell.
Terriers usually have strong characters and are
very tenacious. These dogs frequently dislike
other animals, including other dogs, and often
seem keen to pick an argument.

MUST KNOW

Crossbreeds

A crossbreed is the
result of two pure-
bred dogs of different
breeds mating.
Crossbreeds are
sometimes
deliberately produced
in the hope of
keeping desired
characteristics from
each breed.
Labradoodles
(Labrador crossed
with Poodle) were an
attempt to produce
guide dogs that did
not moult. (A mongrel
– or bitser! – results
from dogs of usually
unknown, mixed
parentage.)

Hounds

This group covers a selection of breeds that is intended for the pursuit of quarry whether by sight or scent. Sight hounds, as the name implies, tend to be very aware of movement, even at some distance. Scent hounds follow their noses and can be difficult to call off the scent once started. These dogs range in size from the small Beagle through to the magnificent Irish Wolfhound.

There is also great variation in shape, from the long-bodied, short-legged Dachshund to the elegant Borzoi. Hounds are also known for their distinctive voices, which are considered melodic by enthusiasts.

▲ Dachshunds have three coat types: the wire-haired (as in this picture), long-coat, and smooth coat. Spirited and plucky, the name means 'badger dog'.

Terriers

These breeds are generally fairly hardy and determined in character. Bred to be busy working dogs originally, some have moved away from this purpose. It is hard to imagine a show Yorkshire Terrier chasing a rat! Coat textures range from silky through to a hard wiry hair. They can be very vocal – originally so that they could maintain contact with the huntsman – and also rather snappy, as they were bred to kill vermin and to bait large animals.

▲ The Airedale is the largest of the Terrier breeds and was once very popular as a service dog prior to the German Shepherd dog.

Working and Pastoral

These groups cover breeds, such as the St Bernard, that have served man in many ways, including herding, tracking, guiding, rescue work and guarding. Breeds in these groups are generally considered to be very trainable as so many of them have always worked closely with their owners. Their high intelligence has brought them many new roles, as assistance dogs for the disabled as well as appearing on screen in films. Bred to work all day, they particularly require owners who will keep them mentally stimulated.

▲ This German Shepherd, a member of the Pastoral group, is normal coated. Long-coated varieties are also popular as pets.

▲ Many of the companion/ toy breeds, like this Lhasa Apso, have long, silky coats that require regular attention, especially as the dog's body lies close to the ground.

▲ Drop ears are a feature of the gundog breeds. Many people find this attractive, as it softens the expression compared to the prick ears of the guarding breeds.

▲ An old favourite, the Dalmatian (made famous by the Walt Disney films), is still loved by both children and adults today.

Companion and Toy

An astounding variety of shapes, coat types and temperaments makes up this enormous group. The one thing these dogs have in common is that they are small. Despite their lack of size, some of them were also intended to be noisy watch dogs, giving warning of possible intruders. Their diminutive size is not reflected in their temperament – they can be a real handful in a small package!

Gundogs

Bred to be hunting companions with a range of roles, all gundogs are usually extremely intelligent and active. As pet dogs, Labradors and Golden Retrievers are probably the most familiar breeds of this group. Their equable temperament is personified by the image of a guide dog for the blind.

The multi-purpose Hunt, Point, Retrieve (HPR) breeds of gundog are probably better known in Europe, although their popularity is slowly spreading around the world.

Utility

A collection of breeds that doesn't seem to quite fit elsewhere! In North America this is called the Non-sporting group. In the UK this group includes some of the Spitz breeds, which have a separate group under FCI (Federation Cynologique Internationale) classification. The Dalmatian appears here along with the Bulldog, Chow Chow and Akita. Many of these breeds had working origins but are seldom seen in those roles today.

Few can imagine the glamorous Poodle as a water retrieving gundog, or realize that the folds of skin on the Shar Pei were hard for an opponent to get a grip on, enabling the Shar Pei to manoeuvre and retaliate when attacked.

Ruling bodies

The groupings we have shown are generalized – the exact classifications vary slightly between the American Kennel Club, the Federation Cynologique Internationale and the Kennel Club of Great Britain, the three main ruling bodies in the purebred dog world. Kennel associations in other countries generally follow similar classifications to one of these. The FCI has the largest number of groups, giving Spitz breeds, as well as Dachshunds, a group of their own,

Lack of logic

The logic by which the breeds are classified is sometimes rather puzzling. Not all small dogs are in the Toy/Companion group, and not all terriers are in the Terrier group. It is only in comparatively recent times that the Kennel Club in the UK divided Working and Pastoral into two groups: one being breeds that were primarily herders and stock guards, the other everything else.

Take time to research

Hopefully you can see the benefit of acquainting yourself with the origins of your chosen pet, as this may affect your approach to training and expectations. These days most planned breeding is to produce pets and show dogs. Very few dogs have the opportunity to fulfill their original function, but the instincts will still be there. Time spent researching in books, magazines and breed clubs, and talking to owners who already have the same breed, will pay dividends.

Virtually all breeds have a breed rescue centre. The Kennel Club has a breed rescue directory (see page 186). If you want a specific breed and want to help a dog in need you could contact the appropriate centre via the KC. The rescue centre may also give you a more honest insight into the true character of the breed and its problems.

(see page 186)

Further choices

By now you may have narrowed your search to one or two of the groups, because you feel they have the characteristics and qualities that you are looking for. Within each group the breeds have a variety of coat types and textures. All dogs must be taught to enjoy being groomed.

Houseproud

Short-haired breeds generally have less coat to shed but it is amazing how difficult the short hairs can be to remove from furniture. Although low maintenance they still need a brush over from time to time; their coats will also benefit from polishing with a chamois. Long, shaggy coats need regular attention, preferably daily, to keep them looking and smelling pleasant. Matts form quickly and if not kept brushed out will need clipping off completely. Done daily, it does not take more than five minutes to run a comb through a long-haired dog.

Some breeds do not shed at all. This can be an important factor if anyone in the family suffers from allergies. Poodles and Bichon Frise both have lovely coats that are soft and attractive. While neither of these breeds moult, they need regular trimming to keep the coat to a manageable length. There is an art to shaping the cut to achieve the classic breed appearance. Many of the trimmed breeds need attention every six or eight weeks.

▼ The Komondor's unique dreadlocks are never brushed or combed, and they do not come out when the dog is bathed. Instead they tighten up with age and washing.

◄ The Pomeranian belongs to the Toy dog group. It has a soft and fluffy undercoat and a thick, stand-off outer coat that requires daily grooming.

This can add up to a considerable cost unless the owner has the facilities and learns to do their own grooming.

Different coat types appear within some breeds – there are long and short coated German Shepherd dogs, for example. Belgian Shepherd dogs have long, short or wiry coat textures. Terriers' wire-haired coats are traditionally hand-stripped, which is not difficult for pet owners to learn if they wish, but does require some time. Spaying and castrating sometimes alters the coat texture, a well-known problem with Cocker Spaniels, who can end up very fluffy.

Large or small
As yet we have not mentioned cost, another unfortunate reality of dog ownership. We are not talking about the cost of buying a dog but of maintaining him in the style that he requires (not necessarily the style to which he'd like to become accustomed!) You don't have to give him the best rump steak, but he will need to eat. There is a vast array of dog foods on the market: dry, semi-moist, frozen, tinned and so on. They vary enormously in price but, generally speaking, the better quality foods are not cheap. Obviously, large dogs will eat more than small dogs so you must consider the cost of feeding.

To some extent your home environment will have a bearing on the size of dog you choose. Some big dogs, such as Greyhounds, do not need the amount of exercise that people always assume. Some small dogs, Jack Russell Terriers for example, require plenty of vigorous exercise to keep them from becoming bored.

Sex and age

Having chosen the breed, it is time to decide whether to buy a dog or a bitch, a puppy or an adult. Many people think bitches make better pets, as dogs are thought to be more territorial. And for some people a cute puppy is a must have!

Considering the sex

Success in training has more to do with the individual dog's character than whether it is male or female. Personal preference also plays its part.

However, there are some practical considerations. For instance, bitches come into season (usually twice a year for roughly three weeks at a time), when they will need to be kept away from male dogs. Being in season can affect a bitch's training, as she may become moody. If you are not going to breed from your bitch, you should consider having her spayed.

Dogs, on the other hand, may show fewer signs of hormonal changes (unless an in-season bitch is around). Male dogs may also have more 'presence', which some people find appealing. Both male and female dogs can make equally

▼ If they are allowed to, male dogs will scent mark by cocking their leg on all trees, lamp-posts and other vertical surfaces. This is not necessary, and as part of house-training they should be encouraged to urinate on command and be discouraged from continual scent marking.

◄ The advantage of opting for a puppy is that it is effectively a 'clean sheet of paper' with no residual bad habits. Older dogs may come with some 'baggage'.

good guard dogs and both can be good with the children, family friends, cats and other pets. Male dogs, however, may be more prone to aggressive behaviour towards the family or other dogs. Castration is not a cure for all behavioural problems but can help in many cases.

Questions of age

Puppies are labour-intensive. They need to eat, relieve themselves and play often, interspersed by sleep. Older dogs need fewer meals and can hold their bladder for longer periods. However, an older dog may find it harder to adapt to a new lifestyle whereas a puppy can be moulded to suit his family. Many people assume an older dog will be house-trained, good to take for walks, come when it is called and be able to be left home alone. Sadly this is often not the case. The dog may not have had any training in his previous environment, which can lead to behavioural problems that need to be overcome before the dog develops into a suitable pet.

MUST KNOW

One to one
Two puppies may not be better than one. If you do opt for two, make sure they look to their owner for fun and companionship, rather than depending on each other. In addition, sibling rivalry may become a major issue at a later stage.

Breeder or rescue?

Ask yourself: where are you going to get your dog? If you opt for a purebred dog, you will need to find a reliable breeder. You may prefer the idea of a rescue dog, but can you really care for an unwanted dog?

Choosing a purebred pup

So you have selected your preferred breed and decided you would like to buy a puppy. A good starting point is the national Kennel Club, where it should be possible to get information on the breed clubs for your selected breed, as well as contact information on breeders. However, bear in mind that you cannot assume that registration is a guarantee of quality.

It is important to find a puppy reared in the right environment, whether this be a 'pet home' or a professional breeder. Choose puppies that have been bred from parents who are fit and healthy and of sound temperament and who

▼ Rescue puppies may still be a clean sheet, assuming staff have been able to spend some time with them. The exact breed, and therefore the appearance of the eventual adult dog, may be down to guess work.

have had health screening appropriate to their breed. If you have concerns about the parents, then don't look at the pups, because all pups look simply adorable!

Puppy expectations

The pups should have been reared with due care and attention to their physical and mental well-being. Whether in the house or outside in a kennel, they should be used to being handled and be accustomed to everyday noises and events. They should have been weaned onto solid food, have been wormed at least once if not more, and may also have had health checks and screening themselves.

All puppies whether purebred or crossbred should be sent off to their new homes with a diet sheet and care instructions. Registered pedigree puppies should also have a pedigree and registration certificate. Where the breeder has put time and effort into rearing the litter, the new owner will see the benefits as their puppy adapts quickly to his new environment and engages in interactive learning with his new family.

Older dogs

Breeders may also have older dogs available sometimes. They can be retired breeding stock or youngsters which they have run on while they decide which one to keep. Hopefully, regardless of age, they will all have had time and effort put into their daily lives, enabling them to make good pets. Bear in mind that they may have lived in kennels all their lives and may not be house-trained, even though they are adult!

Older dogs take longer to settle in. Even if they behave well, you need to spend time teaching basic exercises and maybe tricks, to strengthen the bond between you. It can take up to a year for an adult rescue dog to blossom.

▲ General rescue kennels usually have a selection of dogs of all ages, shapes and sizes. The dogs come from many sources and their backgrounds are frequently unknown.

want to know more?

Take it to the next level...

Go to...
- ▶ why train – pages 24–43
- ▶ starting off – pages 44–57
- ▶ training methods – pages 58–73

Other sources
- ▶ **A local vet or animal sanctuary**
  a great starting point for looking into the right dog for you
- ▶ **Pet food supplier**
  your local pet food shop and garden centre may also have ads for dogs
- ▶ **Internet**
  visit www.the-kennel-club.org.uk

why

train?

Badly-behaved dogs rank highly in lists of things people complain about. You don't want an unruly dog and neither do others. It's up to you to establish the rules of acceptable behaviour. Sound training is the way to achieve this.

Training basics

Unruly dogs are like unruly children – they are a menace to have around. Everyone wants a dog that fits in with their lifestyle and is a pleasure to be with. Unfortunately, puppies are not born ready trained and you will have to put in some effort to achieve that comfortable relationship.

MUST KNOW

Child-friendly?
Even the friendliest dog can pose a danger to a small child if one or both are over-excited and the child gets knocked over. Owners must always be aware that even the most laid-back dog can react in a way that is totally out of character if taken by surprise.

Acceptable behaviour

So what is 'acceptable behaviour' when it comes to dogs? The answer is: whatever is acceptable to the owner. One person may be happy to have the dog sleep on the end of their bed – another would be horrified and find this unacceptable. The proviso to this is that if the dog's behaviour is unacceptable to other people then the owner may have a problem. Very few people will tolerate indiscriminate fouling, excessive noise or intractable behaviour from other people's pets.

Sadly, rescue kennels are always full to overflowing with dogs looking for a new home. While some are in rescue for genuine reasons, too many are there because the relationship between dog and family has broken down, or not reached the family's expectations. In many cases this situation can be prevented by proper training.

Training sessions

Dog training should not be limited to half an hour a day, with your dog left to his own devices for the other twenty three and a half hours. The verbal commands we teach should be useful on many occasions throughout the day, 'stand' for grooming or at the vet, or 'sit' to have the collar and lead put on, or before crossing the road, or getting into or out of the car. Both you and your dog can benefit from the mental stimulation of training sessions. At the same time your one-to-one relationship with your dog will be

strengthened as you learn to communicate with each other. Successful training is a great confidence booster for all dogs and owners, especially those dogs (and people!) with a shy and reserved nature.

Don't forget that dogs are pack animals and they will be more emotionally stable and secure if the boundaries of acceptable behaviour within the family 'pack' have been made clear. This sounds very rigid but it need not be; it is no more severe than insisting that your children be well mannered. Most owners derive great pleasure from having others admire their well-behaved dog.

▲ Family dogs watching while children played in the park on the way home from school used to be a common sight; but thoughtless dog owners and new regulations mean many parks now ban dogs.

MUST KNOW

Frequent recall

Many people make the mistake of only recalling the dog and putting the lead on when they are ready to go home. It does not take a bright dog long to realize this and he may go deaf at the recall request. Sensible owners should recall their dogs frequently, praising them for coming and giving a variety of rewards – maybe a tasty treat, or a game with a special toy, or at other times a pat and cuddle before instructing the dog to go and play again.

▲ You can reward your dog for a prompt response to returning when called, by producing a toy from your pocket and having a short game. Put the toy away again while your dog still wants to play.

Dog training should be fun

You should strive to enjoy a strong relationship with your dog so that, above all, training will be fun for both of you. Some owners enjoy the training so much that they go on to compete in various training competitions with their dogs, meeting people and making new friends along the way. By the same token, you should be the most interesting thing in your dog's life. So many people take their dog to the local park, let him off the lead to run riot with all the other dogs, then put a lead on him again and take him home. As the owner, you should be encouraging your dog to prefer to be with you, using whatever incentives you find necessary.

MUST KNOW

Facing potential problems

So many owners, when they find that they have a problem with their dog wanting to chase joggers or cyclists, go out of their way to avoid meeting the problem. We believe it is much more sensible to confront the issue and teach the dog that his behaviour is inappropriate. Remember, an out-of-control dog is a danger to himself and to others.

WHY TRAIN?

28

Whilst it is nice for your dog to socialize with other dogs, it should not be at the cost of basic control. Free running is great exercise and fun for the dog but should only be allowed once he can respond reliably to you as his owner.

Control of your dog

If the dog will not respond off the lead then it should be kept on the lead for its own and others' safety. More and more public areas are imposing stringent conditions for dog walkers, fencing off sections where dogs are not allowed and expecting owners to clear up after their dogs. In the few areas where children's playgrounds are not fenced off it is vitally important that dogs are kept under control.

It is the most natural thing to take the dog for a walk and the children to play in the park. Common sense says that it is almost impossible to watch both children and dog if they are all running around in different directions. It may be more socially acceptable to keep the dog on the lead however well behaved he is, while supervising children. This can also be an ideal opportunity to practise basic control exercises.

Problem solving
With effort, the trigger that caused your dog's bad behaviour can be switched to produce good behaviour. Spending time with cyclists, for example, allows your dog to learn how he should behave and then you can reward accordingly. This is far more beneficial than avoiding the problem.

▼ However playful and friendly this Retriever's intentions may be towards a passing cyclist, the potential for an accident and injury is obvious. Think ahead of your dog.

Start basic handling

Our training courses assume that owners can handle their dogs, and that means more than just putting on a collar and lead. This may sound a very obvious statement, but it never fails to amaze us how many people say 'I don't do that because he doesn't like it', meaning they cannot touch their dog unless he chooses to let them. No one is suggesting that your dog should submit to being mauled by all and sundry, but it is essential that you and your family are able at the very least to handle him thoroughly for grooming, bathing when necessary, veterinary examinations and so on.

▼ Two alternative methods of checking the dog's feet and nails. Both are correct.

Never too soon

Even though a young puppy may be ticklish and not yet require serious grooming, he should be accustomed to it at an early stage to prevent problems later. It is much easier to gently but firmly insist with an eight week-old puppy than to try the same handling with an eight month-old young adult.

▶ Examine your dog's paws thoroughly between the pads and around the base of the nails. Dew claws should be checked too.

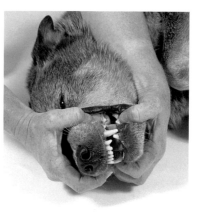

▲ Examine the dog's ears for dirt or foreign bodies regularly.

▲ Your dog should be familiar with having his teeth and mouth checked.

Grooming benefits

A few minutes daily spent brushing the puppy's baby coat, checking his ears, teeth, feet and toenails will pay dividends in the long run. A dog will soon learn to enjoy these one-to-one moments with his owner.

It is worthwhile occasionally to trim or at least go through the motions of trimming his nails. Many dogs do not need their nails clipped because the exercise they get keeps them short. However, in old age most dogs tend to take less exercise and it is not unusual for their nails to need clipping for comfort.

If your dog is not used to this he might get very stressed and unhappy. And if you have just acquired an older or rescue dog, particularly if he is not used to being handled or has unfortunate associations with it, he will need to become accustomed slowly and steadily to the handling. Do not try to do too much at once; very short sessions ending in a reward – even if you have not groomed his entire coat – can be built up over time.

MUST KNOW

Visiting the vet

Sooner or later all dogs need to visit the vet, even if only for booster vaccinations. During these visits the vet will usually give the dog a general health check. If you have already taken the time to handle and groom your dog, and clip his nails, then the visit will be much more pleasant and beneficial for all of you.

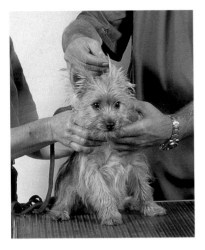

▲ Examination by a vet or groomer can be very stressful. If your dog will not allow you to examine him, what chance has the poor vet?

Grooming and handling

Many dogs particularly dislike having their toe-nails clipped, so owners often hand this problem over to their local vet or dog-groomer. This may be even more stressful for the dog because the vet, or groomer, is obliged to do all four feet in one session.

How much kinder it would be if the owner were to take the time to do, say, one nail a day, each time rewarding with praise and a treat so that it is a pleasant experience. It will not be long before all four feet can be done in one session.

When to say no!

Try to have a positive attitude. If your dog is obviously just about to do something such as chase a cat, or is caught in the act, then by all means say 'no!'; but then try to follow it up immediately with positive commands so that he can be praised. You should use this decisive approach whenever possible as it applies to almost every aspect of the dog's life, from house-training onwards.

Many people tell their dog off long after he has misbehaved, by which time the dog has forgotten about it and does not understand why he is being told off. For example, if an owner comes back from shopping and finds that the dog has chewed the leg of the antique table it is too late to tell him off. Dragging the dog over to point out the damage while scolding him will only confuse him. If the dog learns anything from that, it will be that he should be afraid when his owner returns home.

Caught in the act

However, if a dog is caught in the act of chewing, perhaps on a chair that he shouldn't be on, the owner is justified in reprimanding with a sharp 'no!' and removing him from the chair.

MUST KNOW

Health concerns
If there are any health concerns regarding your dog this can have an effect on how, when and what training he does. If a dog has a medical problem, for example hip dysplasia, where there is a risk of training causing pain, then you must adapt your approach accordingly.

Praising your puppy

The reprimand should stop him instantly, but the owner must also recognize that a puppy has a need to chew on something and must therefore offer a more appropriate chewing toy. So telling the dog off must be followed by giving him something he can chew on, such as his bone or a toy. Then you can praise the puppy for chewing on that.

Whatever your dog may be doing that you do not like, rather than nagging him 'no! no! no!', try to channel his behaviour towards something acceptable so that you can praise him.

▼ This young Labrador has been told off for having a good chew on a seat he shouldn't be on. The owner now offers a treat toy (which can have a tasty morsel placed inside) to help keep the dog interested in the correct chew.

Persistent barking

Another common problem, in which owners inadvertently give the wrong signals to their dogs, is persistent barking. Shouting 'No! Be quiet!' (or something similar) appears to the dog to be confirming the need for noise. Dogs bark for many different reasons, sometimes to warn the household of possible intruders or at least visitors, or perhaps the postman; at other times it is just to seek attention. Most people do want their dog to warn off strangers, but not to excess.

If the reason for barking is justified, you should acknowledge your dog's warning, but then take charge of the situation. Instruct your dog to 'sit' or 'down' quietly by your side, or perhaps command him to go to his bed. This should divert your dog's attention from barking without the need for constant reprimanding. Praise the dog for responding correctly.

Attention seeking

If the dog is barking just to seek attention, then any attention is better than none. Try to look at this from the dog's point of view: he is barking to seek attention; so what happens? You go to your dog, usually to tell him off, but the dog thinks he has 'won' as he has got the attention he wanted, and this has reinforced his impression that you will come when called.

◄ Ignoring your dog totally can be one of your most effective punishments. It may feel strange not to respond to your dog's incessant barking for attention, but by telling him off you are simply heeding his demand.

The best way to deal with this type of barking is to ignore it completely. Initially this may be hard, but if the dog gets no response he will usually cease making a noise. As soon as he is quiet then you can reward him. If the dog is very persistent then, for the sake of the neighbours, it may be necessary to interrupt his behaviour. Ideally this should be something unexpected which makes him pause for breath, such as banging a metal tray. Praise the pause and then focus the dog's attention elsewhere.

Dogs are not humans

Another common problem we come across in our training sessions is that owners insist on treating their dogs as little people and not as dogs. Endowing a dog with human characteristics often causes unnecessary problems in the training process.

Frustrated owners will accuse their dog of bearing a grudge, or complain that he has misbehaved in class to spite them (for a telling off they gave him earlier). This is simply not the case, and when the situation has been reviewed, and seen from the dog's point of view this usually eases the tension and allows training to progress to resolve the conflict.

Affection

Of course we all cuddle our dogs and chat to them, showing them affection which, hopefully, they enjoy. But remember, it is the pleasant tones and obvious attention, rather than the explicit meaning of the words, which makes it seem that they understand everything you say.

As a footnote we would also add that we do not profess to know all the answers to understanding dogs, and even after having helped train thousands of dogs of all breeds, we never stop learning.

▲ Firm and fair handling, together with love and affection, will guide your new dog in the right direction.

MUST KNOW

Praising
Whatever the breed of dog it is natural, especially for a young dog, to see what it can get away with in terms of behaviour. Keep a check on this so that it does not get out of hand, but remember that praising good behaviour is more beneficial than punishing bad.

How dogs learn

Dogs learn by trial and reward. If they do something by accident or design and get a pleasant result then they are more likely to repeat the behaviour. If there is no reward, or they are scolded, they are less likely to repeat it. Try to create situations that present opportunities for reward.

Trial and reward

You need to find out what motivates your dog, what he likes and what will get him to respond to your training best. You need to show him that responding well to your training brings rewards. Thankfully puppies and most adult dogs are willing to please, and this can be cultivated as they learn to look to you for guidance.

Whether your dog is an extrovert, or shy and reserved, the principle of trial and reward is the same. The extrovert will probably experience more learning situations as he rushes in head-first but will recover quickly from any setbacks. The shy dog will be more cautious in his approach and will usually take longer to recover. The sensible owner will try to introduce his dog to as many non-threatening situations as possible to widen the dog's horizons and build his confidence.

Learning curve

As instructors, one of the most rewarding aspects of taking training classes is seeing introverted dogs blossom, with positive handling, into much happier characters. This learning curve is not dependent on any formal training. The puppy that falls into the water bowl and does not like the experience will tend to be more careful next time, whereas the puppy who found it great fun splashing around in the water will be permanently wet.

MUST KNOW

Seek a balance
Most children, if asked, would like an endless supply of sweets, unlimited television and computer games, and to go to bed when they liked. But sensible parents realize that this would be detrimental in the long term and so try to steer a course between praise for good behaviour and ignoring any attention seeking.

Art of training
Frustrating though it may be, you should always praise your dog for returning, and if there is an art to dog training it is in being able to say 'Good dog, you little *******!' in a sincerely happy tone with a smile on your face.

▼ Puppies should be handled gently and frequently. They should be accustomed to being restrained quietly, but firmly, so that if it should be necessary for them to have, say, veterinary treatment they will not find this unduly stressful.

We can harness this learning by using trial and reward in our training. The key is to reward favourably the behaviour which you want, as it is then likely to be repeated. This does not mean spoiling your dog with endless unearned treats and never telling him off. What it does mean is using a combination of food treats, plenty of affection when you want to give it, and dedicated time for play.

How to tell off

A reward or chastisement needs to be tailored to the individual dog – and at the appropriate time (for example immediately the behaviour occurs). A common occurrence is the dog that does not return when called. Eventually the dog does return only to be greeted with a severe scolding. The owner is scolding the dog for not coming back when called, but in the dog's mind he is being scolded for coming back.

Dogs do not generally think or reason like humans (contrary to popular belief); they associate being told off with what they are doing now, not with what they did earlier. Therefore even the dog who is totally innocent can be made to appear guilty by an owner's body language and harsh voice.

WHY TRAIN?

37

Body language

Dogs can be very vocal animals, but they also use their bodies in many different ways to communicate to each other and to us. Understanding body language is crucial.

Picking up signals

Dogs are much more aware of body language than their owners are: one only has to see an older experienced dog appear to anticipate his owner's instructions. In fact, what has usually happened is that the dog has recognized the body language and knows what instructions are coming. Changes in attitude are frequently picked up by the dog regardless of the owner's intentions. Many owners comment to us that their dogs know when they are happy or sad.

▶ Puppies solicit food from their mothers and other adult dogs by licking at their mouths so food is regurgitated. Such behaviour clearly indicates to this mature dog (right) that the younger dog is only a baby and poses no threat.

Posture and stance

Body language, to your dog, is your posture and stance, which he interprets rightly or wrongly. The dog who appears 'guilty' when the owner arrives home to find his slippers destroyed would appear just as guilty if the owner came storming in annoyed after a bad journey home.

In the first instance the owner would interpret the dog's lowered posture, wagging tail and fawning behaviour as 'knowing he was guilty'. In the second case the same behaviour on the part of the dog would probably be interpreted by the owner as sympathy for his bad day. If only owners were as observant as their dogs.

Reaction dictates response

Many of the behavioural traits of dogs have been well illustrated in television programmes about wolves. Although some of these signals have been toned down in the domestic dog, many are recognizably the same.

The subtle differences in posture and behaviour, which indicate how your dog is feeling, are frequently missed altogether or misread. For example, a puppy with his hackles up from his ears to the base of his tail is usually frightened rather than aggressive. The owner's reaction can dictate the dog's response.

Heed warnings

Dogs rarely 'suddenly' bite. Usually there will have been many warning signs, such as low growls if the dog has been moved off the settee, or a stiff, momentarily frozen stance over the food bowl as the owner comes near. Also be wary of increasing possessiveness of toys with excessive 'play-biting'. These signs, together with a reluctance to do as requested unless it suits him, should be heeded.

Reading signs
Dogs learn from their mothers and siblings and then try to apply these learned interpretations to their dealings with people. They try to read our body language before they associate it with a verbal command. Hopefully any previous owners will have smiled and handled them in a kind and pleasant manner, making calm, friendly sounds at the same time.

▲ The larger dog exudes confidence from his slowly wagging tail to his arched neck, and gives every indication that he is in charge. The younger female dog responds to the larger dog's head above her by lying down.

MUST KNOW

Playgroups
Puppy kindergartens are becoming more popular for developing puppy social skills and starting both puppy and owner off on the right foot.

Learning from mothers

There are many excellent books on inherited and learned behaviour in dogs. Our book is about training rather than behaviour, but you should realize that both these types of behaviour occur and can be channelled to your advantage.

Dogs start to develop their understanding of canine body language while still with their mother and the rest of the litter. The rough play that puppies indulge in teaches them how to behave with each other.

This might seem to be stating the obvious, but it is through this play that a dog learns to communicate with his own kind.

Problem pups

Because of lack of sibling play, puppies who have been taken from the nest too early, or are only pups, may develop problems. They have missed the opportunity to interact with their peer group and thus can lack the skills to communicate with other dogs. A bitch who is a good mother can help alleviate this as she feeds, cares for and plays with her offspring.

◀ The younger female dog has submitted totally, rolling over in front of the more mature dog, ears back accepting his position. Her tail is tucked but wagging to show that she wants to be friendly and is not looking for an argument or a telling off.

Puppy learning

If you are concerned that your dog will not like you if you are firm, then watch a bitch disciplining her boisterous pups. When a puppy has done something the bitch does not like – perhaps nipped her too hard – she bowls the offender over, her upright stance and body posture giving every impression that she is about to kill him. The puppy becomes a picture of submission – on his side or back, legs in the air, ears back, avoiding eye-contact, tail probably between his legs and possibly even urinating as well.

Interaction

As time goes on the puppy learns to read the signals, so all the bitch needs to do is to give a look and the puppy will understand completely. A particularly pushy puppy may keep testing to see what he can get away with, and require more lessons from his mother before he will comply. Once he has left his mother, the puppy needs to continue interacting with other dogs if he is to maintain these social skills.

Getting down to your dog's level

Most people tend to crouch down to meet a puppy. This has the effect of making the person appear smaller and less threatening to the puppy. When you call your puppy, your raised voice, intended to carry the sound, together with your upright posture, may be intimidating. If he appears hesitant as he looks towards you, crouch down, speak in a soft, encouraging voice and hopefully he will come running.

Dealing with a cheeky puppy

The cheeky, confident puppy who comes flying back when called only to stop a few feet in front of you, is a different problem (to the hesitant, worried dog). His body language says it all: tail wagging, head cocked to one side and whites of his eyes showing. He will also often drop into a 'play bow' with his front end down and his tail in the air. It is quite evident that he is saying 'Chase me!' If you are silly enough to take a step towards him he will either back off a few paces or be off, ears back, tail between his legs doing circuits around you in great glee before he returns to start the game again.

Resist the urge

Do not be tempted to launch yourself at him: you might succeed the first time you try but the puppy will learn to be faster next time. The more you flail your arms about and shout, the more fun the puppy believes you are having. Try to keep calm, and if you have a toy or titbit, produce it and try to lure him in. Do not grab him, but make sure that you do not relinquish the toy or titbit until you have hold of his collar.

Some puppies continue to avoid contact in favour of a hoped-for game. Try to ignore such behaviour and walk away avoiding eye contact. Usually your uninterested posture will make him come chasing after you to see why you do not want to play anymore. That is the time to crouch down again and encourage him in, maybe with the toy or titbit. Although this is considered chiefly to be puppy-related behaviour, such goings-on are also frequently seen in older dogs and should be dealt with in exactly the same manner.

▶ A play-bow pose is an easy-to-read example of a dog's body language. The dog is saying quite simply 'chase me!'.

◀ Small children can be easily knocked over and hurt by an exuberant dog, whatever size it is. Children and dogs should never be left unsupervised. What starts as a game can so easily end in tears.

MUST KNOW

Supervision
Even children who are not frightened need to be watched at all times when they are playing with dogs.

Children and dogs

Many of the problems between children and dogs develop because neither understand the body language of the other. Youngsters get over-excited, move rapidly and unexpectedly and scream in high-pitched tones. Dogs often interpret these noises as invitations to play when in fact the child may be fearful. Similarly, a dog's attempts to play and 'be friends' can be seen by the child as an attack.

A dog will usually try to lick the child's face as he would another dog (a small dog may have to jump up), and such actions can increase the child's fear. An exciting game of chase nearly always ends with the child being knocked over, and the dog then believes that the child's howls of distress are an indication of how much fun he is having and jumps on top of him, thus making matters worse. So both dog and child need to be supervised to prevent misunderstandings.

want to know **more?**

Take it to the next level...

Go to...
▶ **Training methods** – pages 58–73
▶ **Weekly training** – pages 74–141
▶ **Using rewards** – pages 152–159

Other sources
▶ **Your local dog training classes**
  A great way to train your dog and be sociable too
▶ **Friends and family**
  Ask those around you with dogs for training tips that really work
▶ **Internet**
  visit www.dogtraining-online.co.uk or www.dogstuff.co.uk or www.companyofanimals.co.uk

starting

off

Little and often is the key to successful training, especially when your dog is young. Begin training with lots of short sessions and plenty of praise, and make sure you always end on a positive note.

Getting started

Whether you realize it or not, you start to teach your dog from the moment you bring him home. Your new arrival will be taking in everything about you – from your appearance to your scent and the sound of your voice.

Use food

If you have a puppy, training can start straight away, but the emphasis is primarily on reward. Puppies tend to be stomachs on legs, so food is the major incentive at this stage. Food treats should be small and tasty so they will be eaten quickly. Small means bite-sized morsels which can almost be swallowed whole. The ideal is small cubes of cheese or diced sausages.

Positive steps

If you have acquired a puppy you should start by teaching him his name, then how to be clean in the house, and also the difference between good and bad. Avoid being negative – some puppies end up thinking their name is 'no!'. Instead, take a positive attitude as outlined in Chapter One, as this can make your dog's introduction to his new home much easier.

Acclimatizing your puppy

Before beginning any formal training, try to cultivate habits that will stand you and your dog in good stead for the future. The puppy's inclination is to be with someone, so make use of this by calling his name, commanding 'come' and praising 'good dog' as he does. Patting, a titbit and a game will build up pleasant associations in his mind with being called.

On their first outings to the park most people want to keep their puppy on the lead in case they lose him. If the area is secure it is much more sensible to let the puppy off the lead and encourage him to follow you.

At a young age the puppy is generally looking for leadership and is afraid of losing you, so he will keep check of where you are. Any hesitancy to come when called can usually be rectified by crouching down and offering encouragement, or moving as if to run away.

The puppy must be praised and rewarded for coming, to make it worth his while.

Formal training time

Young puppies have a very short concentration span and tire easily, therefore they should not really attend a formal training class until they are older. However, puppy playgroups are becoming more common and can be great fun as well as enormously beneficial for the pups.

Older pups of 18 weeks or so (depending on the individual and breed) are better able to cope with training sessions. Strong-willed puppies, especially, may need firmer discipline and may be ready for formal training sessions. Bear in mind that however well behaved the puppy, it is not unusual for him to go through a 'teenage rebellion'. Nevertheless, sensibly handled puppies will mature into happy and well-adjusted adult characters.

▲ Remember that all dogs are different and that concentration span can vary within breeds as well as with age. More repetition of training may be required with slower learners, but they will get there in the end.

The case for more training

Contrary to the well-known saying, older dogs can be taught new tricks. You may decide, for whatever reason, that your dog needs more training. Perhaps circumstances have changed, for example a new baby in the family, and previously tolerated behaviour becomes unacceptable. It can be quite a shock to the dog to have the rules altered.

If the changes are to be major, for example restricting his freedom of the house, they may be easier to implement if they occur following other alterations to his routine. If he has been in kennels or you have just moved house, this can be an ideal opportunity to set up a new regime.

MUST KNOW

Freedom at last

An adolescent dog who has never been let off the lead might be much harder to recall when he has his first taste of freedom. After work on a long line (see page 149) a secure area for the first time this happens is recommended.

▲ A rescue dog's appearance is not necessarily a guide to his temperament – even small dogs can be quite ferocious.

Rescue dogs

Rescue dogs of any age are usually of an unknown background and may have experienced some degree of trauma. This can mean that, instead of starting with a clean sheet, you may have to cope with unacceptable behaviours already established. An even greater degree of patience, understanding and consistency may be required on your part.

Establish a regular routine

While it is nice to allow the dog time to settle in his new home, it is advisable to adhere to clear rules from the beginning. A regular routine should help him settle more quickly. You may need to think carefully about how he is handled and approached. It may be easy to insist with an eight-week-old puppy, but it would be foolhardy to try and insist straight away with a large, adult dog.

Circumnavigating the issue in the early stages may help break the bad habit. For example, if he stakes a claim to your settee or double bed and refuses to budge without an argument, it may be more sensible not to allow the dog access in the future.

As he settles in and you begin to understand each other, he should accept that when you say 'move' you mean it. This is not going to happen overnight. Some dogs will accept this more quickly than others.

MUST KNOW

Dealing with rescue dogs

It is worth pointing out that most rescue dogs follow a normal pattern regarding settling in to their new home. The first week or two they are usually on their best behaviour, then they test the water and show their true colours. If this can be worked through, they settle down securely in their new home.

Indoor kennels

The arrival on the scene of collapsible dog crates or indoor cages was frowned upon by many people in the dog world who did not understand their use. They were never intended to be a 'cage' that the dog lived in permanently or as a punishment. But if used correctly they are a versatile training aid, helping to protect the dog from possible danger, such as electric cables, as well as protecting the house and contents from demolition. They are also helpful during house-training. Most designs will fold flat and can be moved easily and erected in the car or in a hotel or friend's house when required.

Using a crate as a bed

If introduced in a considerate way, most dogs will quickly come to view their crate as a happy, safe den. Whenever the dog is put in the crate, give him a small treat and tell him 'bed', to make it a pleasant experience. Our older dogs, who have not needed to be crated for many years will joyfully take up residence if the crate is erected, wagging their tails waiting for a treat. The crate should be large enough for the dog to stand up and turn around in comfortably.

▼ They may look very similar in colouring and size but each puppy has its own unique character. Even if two apparently identical puppies go to the same home, they will still develop as individuals in their own right.

▲ Folding crates are a very versatile tool in dog training, as well as keeping the dog, or puppy, safe and secure. While to us it may look like a cage, correctly introduced it soon becomes his den.

Buying a crate

It is advisable if buying a crate for your new puppy to get the size which will accommodate him as an adult if necessary. This will mean that as a puppy there will be plenty of room for a comfortable bed with a chew toy and room for newspaper in case he has an accident.

And so to bed...

Do resist buying an expensive, attractive bed for a puppy as he will probably have great fun chewing it to pieces. Cardboard boxes come in a range of sizes and it is not nearly so upsetting or expensive when you find them in bits!

Sufficient space for newspaper is particularly important for nights. Most puppies, if put to bed very late and taken out very early, quickly learn to be clean overnight. Ideally, during the day, the dog will only be shut in for short periods of time when it is not practical to supervise him properly.

MUST KNOW

Without a crate
The crate can be dispensed with and replaced by a comfortable dog bed once the puppy or the rescue dog settles in and can be trusted loose in the house.

Never send the dog to bed as a punishment or he will resent going there. Going to his bed should be a positive, pleasant experience before he gets into trouble. It should not take long for the dog to view his crate or bed as a safe den.

House training

Young puppies need to relieve themselves frequently – on waking up after a short nap, after eating and often during play. It is pointless with a very young puppy to put him outside, shut the door in his face and expect him to go to the toilet. The pup will usually just sit looking up to the door, waiting for the owner to come out and play as well.

Time spent in the first few days going outside with the puppy, and praising him while he performs, will ensure rapid house training. In the early days and weeks it is unrealistic to expect your puppy to 'ask' to go outside. It is really up to the owner to realize 'that it is probably time' and take the puppy outside. While praising the dog as he performs, use a word or phrase like 'hurry up' or 'be clean'. The puppy will soon make the association between the word and his action. This can be extremely useful later on.

MUST KNOW

Kid-free zone
While the puppy should not be allowed to predominate, it is essential that children in particular are taught that even the dog has a right to some peace and quiet in his crate or bed.

◀ The dog who understands the command 'Bed' can be kept from getting under your feet.

Equipment and training aids

The essential tool is you, the trainer, working one-to-one with your dog. Training aids are anything which will help you. Your hands and voice, food treats, lead, collar, clicker and toys are all tools you can use.

Getting to know you

The methods explained in this book are the ones that we use and teach on our courses, and which we have found work well for the majority of dogs. We recommend that you start teaching your dog on a one-to-one basis because dog training is a bit like learning a foreign language. Different tones of voice, timing and accents make it harder for the dog to understand what is required. Once he has started to understand then others can work with him, using the same set of commands.

In dog training a dog is customarily worked on the owner's left-hand side and for the purposes of this book it is assumed that is where your dog will be.

▶ You should be appropriately dressed. Wear comfortable clothing and flat shoes. It is important that you are not worrying about soiling your clothes with dirty paws or getting jewellery caught up in your dog's teeth or feet.

▲ A 2m (6ft) double-clipped leather training lead (1) can be useful, but a good 1m (3–4ft) leather lead is ideal for training (2). Nylon (3,4), rope (5), or canvas (6) are also suitable. A ring in the handle will enable the lead to be kept short with ease for close work, by clipping the trigger hook onto the ring before attaching to the collar. A split ring, such as a key-ring, can be fitted if the lead does not already have one. Under certain circumstances, extending leads (7), head collars and harnesses can also be useful.

Voice

Your voice is your link to your dog. It commands, praises or scolds. When you begin training, make your commands firmly but nicely. You do not have to shout at your dog to make him understand. When you say your dog's name say it nicely, when you praise him be enthusiastic, when you scold more or less growl at him.

Praise

Praising your dog is the most important part of training. It is the best way to let him know he has done well. Praise warmly and pat him as his primary reward. The praise should be geared towards the individual dog's temperament. If he is very excitable then praise him calmly, but if he is reticent then you should aim to make the praise more dynamic.

MUST KNOW

Training tools

Wherever possible use tools that will enable you and your dog to succeed in a way that is pleasant and enjoyable for both of you.

▲ Check chains come in a variety of weights, lengths and shapes of link but they all do the same job: a long link (1), a medium-weight flat link (2), a fine flat link (3). They should only be used for the purposes of training.

Hands

Your hands show the dog what to do: they will teach, praise and correct him. Your dog should enjoy the physical contact and feel complete trust in your hands.

Be patient, firm and kind

The virtues of patience, firmness and kindness are ones that you need in order to train your dog. To train your dog successfully, remember to employ these three essentials in equal measures. Keep in mind also that a well-trained dog is not an instant commodity.

Giving commands

This does not mean screaming instructions at your dog nor being a bully; it does mean, however, being firm and fair. Dogs like to know the rules. Remember, a command is an instruction not a request, and is not optional.

Commands must be given clearly and you must avoid confusion. Say 'sit' not 'sit down', which is two commands at once and will confuse a trained dog. 'Sit' is 'sit' and 'down' means 'lie flat on the floor'. 'Off', for example, could mean either 'do not jump up' or 'get off the settee'.

Listen to the rest of the family; if they all tend to say 'sit down' and 'down' means 'do not jump up', then it may be easier to teach everyone a new command. You could make 'flat' mean 'lie down on the ground'. Ultimately it does not really matter what the commands are so long as they are used consistently. It is also the tone not the volume that is important.

It is just as important to let the dog know when an exercise has been completed. Use a release word or phrase such as 'that will do' or 'that's it', not 'good dog', or he may move whenever you try to praise him.

'Good dog' means 'keep doing what you are doing, it is right'; it does not mean 'you have finished and it's okay to run around'.

Time out

If you are having a bad day and everything seems to be going wrong or you're coming down with 'flu, then leave the training alone. The occasional day missed will not hurt, but if you find you are missing every other day then you cannot expect to progress. Similarly, do not expect the dog's co-operation and enjoyment if he has a full tummy after dinner, is overly tired, needs to relieve himself or is feeling off colour.

Mistakes become habits

We have a saying in our training sessions that goes: 'once is a mistake, twice is a habit'. If you allow your dog to repeat a mistake continually during an exercise, it will become a habit. When we teach our training classes, we emphasise the need to be precise and to expect and obtain a prompt response from the dog.

▲ The check chain should be long enough to slide comfortably over the dog's head, but when pulled tight should have only 5–10cm (2–4in) of chain up to the end of the lead.

▲ With the dog at the left side, put the collar over the dog's head, so that the chain goes from the lead over the back of the dog's neck and returns underneath. When fitted this way, the chain can tighten and fall loose.

▲ If you fit a check chain upside down by mistake, the chain will tighten but cannot then be slackened on the dog's neck. You must remove the chain and put it back on the correct way round.

Passing the test

We liken learning to train your dog to learning to drive. You are expected to sit up very straight in a car, hold your hands just so on the steering wheel, concentrate, look in the mirrors before indicating, manoeuvring and so on. After passing the driving test (aside from relief) you tend to get more 'relaxed' about driving – while never compromising on safety and competence. We apply the same attitude to our training. If you allow sloppy responses in the early stages then you cannot expect a quick and accurate response at a later stage.

Start as you mean to go on: give one command, help your dog give the correct response, then praise him. Do not keep repeating the command. Always be ready to help the dog respond instantly so that praise can be given and a good habit formed. At all times in training you must show, teach and reward.

▶ Half-check collars are useful as everyday collars as well as for training. The collars illustrated – leather (1) and nylon (2,3) – are all adjustable, and useful for growing dogs.

▼ Everyday collars can have buckle or clip fastenings. They can come in nylon with clip fastening (1), flat leather (2, 6), canvas (3), rolled leather (4), or nylon with a buckle fastening (5).

▲ For a correct half-check collar fit, when the loose ring on the chain is pulled tight, the two ends of the neck strap should be about an inch apart on the dog's neck.

▲ In this half-check collar position the two ends are too close together. Check chains should never be left on an unattended dog or used as an everyday collar.

Collars

Baby puppies should have a closely fitting buckled or clipped collar. It should be tight enough to allow only two fingers to be squeezed underneath it, otherwise the dog will be able to slide free. Age, size and temperament will have a bearing on which collar is most appropriate. Some placid dogs may continue to wear a correctly fitted buckle-type collar. More boisterous dogs may move on to a half-check which gives a greater degree of control but is less demanding than a check chain. We mostly use a half-check or a check chain. If your dog needs a check chain, it should be the size he needs now, not the one he is expected to grow into.

Using a lead

When a lead is attached to a half-check or a check chain, the collar must be kept loose around the dog's neck. Apart from being cruel, your dog cannot learn if the collar is tight around his neck all the time. The lead should be comfortable for you to work with and an appropriate weight for your size of dog.

want to know **more?**

Take it to the next level...

Go to...
▶ **Training methods** – pages 58–73
▶ **Weekly training** – pages 74–141
▶ **Using rewards** – pages 152–159

Other sources
▶ **Friends and family**
  ask around for equipment you can beg or borrow
▶ **On-line auctions**
  you'll probably pick up some great bargains on the internet
▶ **Internet**
  visit www.doggiesolutions.co.uk or www.dogclub.co.uk or www.dogbasics.co.uk

training

methods

All dogs learn at different rates and are motivated by different things. Our training programme is based on reward, be it praise alone, or a combination of food, toys and a clicker.

Rewarding your dog

In theory there are many different methods of dog training. In practice there is a great deal of overlap between them. Praise can be used, plus food or toys, or toys can be used instead of food. Ultimately, the object of the exercise is to reward your dog in a manner that suits him.

Timing is the trick

If there is a trick to dog training, whatever the method, we believe that it is in the timing of the correction and praise. The correction, if required, needs to be applied at the precise moment that the mistake occurs. This should be sufficient to deter your dog, and can then be followed promptly by praise, and we mean praise. Training should be fun for you and the dog, and should not be looked upon as a chore which needs to be done.

Praising your dog

Everyone likes to be praised for a job well done and dogs are no exception. Though they do not understand the exact meaning of the words, dogs very easily understand the tone of them. Therefore the praise must sound genuine even though your patience may have worn a bit thin. Hearing the pleasure and enthusiasm in your voice is one of the prime motivators for your dog.

Getting the right pitch

As already mentioned, your voice and hands are a natural link to your dog. You do not have to make a conscious effort to remember to pick them up and take them with you! The gentle tone of your voice can calm a boisterous dog or give confidence and reassurance to a timid dog. It can also indicate to your dog that he has done something wrong.

MUST KNOW

What is praise?
For many dogs a quiet word and a pat from their owner makes them squirm with delight; but others would sell their souls for a tasty treat. One thing is certain: if the method you use works, do not try to change it.

▶ A quiet moment with dog and owner enjoying physical contact and relaxing in between exercises. You should always take time out just to appreciate contact and companionship with your dog.

Tone of voice

Women usually have an advantage when praising as they tend to have a greater range of pitch. However, they can lack the lower tone for reprimand. Men have the opposite problem and lack the higher pitch for praise. Again we should stress that we are talking about tone not volume.

A dog's hearing is more acute than ours, therefore if he is only a lead's length away you do not need to shout at him. If you shout when he is close by, what are you going to do if he is some 180m (200yd) away? Keeping your voice down encourages him to pay attention, especially if you follow up with an action, whether that be patting, playing or training.

Toys and games

You should be able to play with your dog without need for a toy. Some dogs like to play 'catch my toes', others enjoy a more physical game of 'push and shove'. You should be able to start and stop games when you choose, and certainly not leave it up to the dog to dictate when to play.

Respect... and lack of it

Owners who have a good relationship with their dog usually find that their dog respects them and delights in praise and attention whenever it is offered. The opposite of this is the dog who has little or no respect for a doting owner who smothers the dog with verbal and physical praise, which he has done nothing to deserve.

▲ You, as owner, should always be your dog's favourite playmate, but it's also important that he learns to socialize with other dogs.

Mutual respect

A dog that demands attention when he wants it, and walks away from it when he has had enough, or is outdoors in a park and sees everything else as more interesting than his owner, obviously lacks respect. A dog should always find it more rewarding to interact with his owner, and to take pleasure in being part of the family pack.

Owners enjoy their dogs' company, so pleasure in stroking and talking to them is natural. However, owners should avoid going over the top, babbling incessantly morning, noon and night so the dog no longer listens. He may end up responding better to food, toys or a clicker than to his owner.

◄ This puppy is lying on his back, feet in the air in a submissive position, having his tummy tickled. He is learning his owner is in charge. All puppies should learn to accept and adopt this position.

TRAINING METHODS

Unsure/naughty?
Reprimanding the
unsure dog causes
confusion and loss of
trust. Try to recognize
the difference between
unsure and naughty.
Even if he has
responded correctly
once or twice, this
does not necessarily
mean that he
understands the
command.

Praise step by step

Another advantage of the praise method is that
it is very easy to reward each small step in the
right direction. A gentle pat and word of praise,
given at the right time for each part of an
exercise, soon leads to a dog being confident in
his understanding of the whole exercise.

As we have stressed before (see page 55),
'good dog' should signify to the dog that he is
doing the right thing and should continue, not
that he is being released to play. You should
have a clear word or phrase which will make it
plain to the dog that he has finished the exercise
and may move. It does not matter what words
or phrase you use – 'that will do', 'that's it', 'okay'
or whatever comes most easily to mind is fine –
so long as you try to be consistent.

Ignore early mistakes

While your dog is learning, try to ignore any
mistakes he makes. Instead, help him to
succeed so that you can praise him. If the
mistake is one of anticipation in his enthusiasm
to try to please, then do not get cross, as you
may put him off completely. Gently correct the
mistake and carry on the training.

However, if he is deliberately being defiant,
a sharp verbal rebuke is generally all that is
required. You should then continue the
exercise, helping him so
that praise can be
given.

◄ This young dog's
body posture shows
his delight as the
owner initiates
a game. No toys or
treats are being used,
just mutual pleasure
in the contact with
each other.

TRAINING METHODS

63

Using a clicker

Clicker training has been around for many years. It has its roots in dolphin training in the USA, from where it evolved.

Communication tool

The clicker is a tool that helps you communicate with your dog, without using verbal commands in the early stages. Once your dog understands what he must do and the behaviour has been given a name – 'sit', 'down', and so on – the clicker can be dispensed with, unless needed to teach something new.

How it works

The basic principle is that the noise, the 'click', indicates to the dog that he has done something right. The noise is then followed by a reward, usually food or a toy. One of the advantages of clicker training is that food doesn't have to be given at the same moment as the click.

▲ The clicker is a small plastic device with a metal strip inside which, when pressed and released, makes a clicking noise – hence the name.

▶ When starting clicker training, keep quiet and concentrate on watching the dog so the click is given at the right moment. This will improve your sense of timing as well as encouraging your dog to look at you while he is not being given a continuous verbal signal.

This means that the dog can be told, while at a distance from you, that he has done something correctly, and he can then return for the reward.

Ideal for indulged dogs

Properly taught, the dog will learn that he can earn rewards and he will look for ways to do so. This is enormously beneficial with dog owners who have dogs that pay them little heed – owners who talk to and fuss over their dogs excessively, so much so, in fact, that the words and patting have ceased to have any great value to their dogs. A dog must learn to associate the click with the reward, and for simplicity, we shall discuss this using food.

Clicker with food treats

Treats should be tiny and tasty, so your dog can have lots of them without filling up. Some dogs are happy to work for some of their complete dried food, especially just before meal time. Remember to watch your dog's weight and adjust his meals if needs be to allow for treats. Keep treats on the side, or in a pocket, but not in the hand as a continual lure.

Start with a click, then give your dog a treat, and repeat this five or six times. Do this in different places, as you do not want your dog to think this only happens in one spot. The next time you click, wait to see if your dog actively looks for a treat. If he does then he has made the connection and you can move on. Using the click indicates the end of your dog's action, so do not repeat 'click, click, click' to try and get him to continue doing something such as 'stay'.

If you are expecting your dog to complete an exercise made up of many parts, then each bit will need to be taught, and clicked, as separate exercises first. Then they can be strung together and clicked once at the end of the 'string'.

TRAINING METHODS

String of steps
When teaching things like heelwork, you may expect your dog to sit at heel, look at you, step off with you, keep at heel, sit when you stop and look up at you before being released. You would need to teach your dog each step at a time.

Teaching the 'sit'

Once the link between the click and the treat has been established, you can start using the clicker to train the dog and the sit is a good first exercise, since dogs sit naturally anyway. Either wait for your dog to sit of his own accord and then click and give a treat, or lure him with a treat in your hand for the first time or two. A treat held above his head and moved slightly back will usually get him to sit.

Do not give verbal signals, but click once and then toss the treat so that your dog moves out of the 'sit'. (If you reward him in the 'sit', he may decide not to move and just wait for more.)

Having moved, your dog will probably come sniffing around looking for more treats. Wait to see if your dog shows any signs of sitting.

▶ Another training aid that can been used with clicker training is the target stick (a lightweight pole). This effectively works as an extension of the owner's arm. Whenever the dog touches the tip of the target stick with his nose he gets a click and treat.

If not, he may need to be lured to help him make the connection between action, click and reward. Toss the treat in different directions and move about, so the dog responds to you and not to the location. Once he is doing the 'sit' reliably, then you can add the verbal command. With each command you teach, make sure your dog is confident of doing the correct action before you give it a name.

Teaching other commands

Once your dog is offering to sit promptly after each treat, then the time is right to wait for him to adopt a 'stand', 'down' or other position. Initially he will be confused because now, if he comes and offers to sit, you will ignore him. He will probably try it a few times and may look very puzzled. If he does not attempt to offer a 'stand' or a 'down' then it may be necessary to lure him into one. In a few short sessions, your dog will have realized that he can 'earn' treats and will try and work out what you require him to do.

▼ Once the dog is used to touching the end of the target stick, he can be induced to turn in circles, figures of eight and so on.

Food and toys

You can use food or toys as bonus rewards for your dog, in conjunction with verbal praise. Many people would like to think that using toys and food as treats are totally separate training methods. In reality, there are many similarities.

Mix'n'match

Dogs are motivated by many different things and the key to success is finding the one or ones to suit your dog. As with children, dogs can get bored with being given the same treat all the time, so a variety is much more interesting to them.

Bite-size morsels

Food treats should be very small and tasty so they can be eaten quickly. Small means bite-size morsels which can almost be swallowed whole. Do not waste time giving large treats, which more fussy dogs will take ages to finish, while greedy dogs will become obsessed with looking for crumbs on the ground. The ideal is small cubes of cheese or diced sausages.

Another treat loved by many dogs is cat biscuits, especially if they think they have stolen them from the cat. They are a handy size for most breeds, can be carried loose in the pocket without too much mess and are readily available.

▼ This young crossbred terrier still has his milk teeth. Care must be taken not to be overly rough while playing with this toy, called a ragger. Although it is normal for the milk teeth to fall out, you do not want him to lose them too soon.

◄ This adult German Shepherd is relishing a vigorous tug-of-war game with his owner. They are using a hard ball on a rope which the dog will release on command. The owner can then throw the ball, which the dog will be keen to retrieve so the game can continue.

If you are using lots of food treats, take care to watch your dog's weight. It is quite surprising how quickly small treats can add up in terms of calories (as unfortunately many trainers know!)

Safe and handy toys

Toys can be almost anything that your dog likes to play with provided they are safe and handy to use. The age and breed of your dog will also have a bearing on the preferred toy.

Puppies who still have milk teeth are generally better off with a soft toy as a hard one can hurt their gums and knock their teeth out. When the puppy is teething it is possible that his mouth will be very sore and he may not want to play with any type of toy.

MUST KNOW

Tug toys
A 'tug' with a ball on a rope or a rope ragger can become one of a dog's favourite games. We believe that it can be of great benefit in training – provided the owner can stop the game, with the dog relinquishing the toy on request.

Giving rewards
Whether using food or toys, initially, the reward may need to be very obvious. You might hold it in your hand and use it often. As you progress, still use it frequently but produce it from your pocket. Ultimately the treat becomes incidental because the good behaviour patterns you have taught have become second nature.

Progress to harder toys

Having adult teeth doesn't mean the puppy will stop chewing, though harder toys may be best now. A dog that has never chewed before may go through a 'chewing phase' while the adult teeth bed down in the gums. If appropriate toys are supplied, this phase will wear off.

Special training toys

Your dog can have a selection of toys of his own to chew on and play with whenever he likes; but training toys should not be left lying around for him to play with as he pleases. Training toys should belong to the owner who will determine where, when and for how long they will be played with. This means they will retain their novelty value in the dog's eyes.

▼ This dog is waiting expectantly for the treat reward after sitting promptly when asked. Toys or food may also be used as random rewards for especially good behaviour, or if teaching new exercises.

TRAINING METHODS

70

Play retrieve

Many dogs have a basic instinct to chase a moving object. As puppies, this instinct is motivated by curiosity and a desire to play. Even something as simple as a leaf blowing in the breeze will produce the reaction of chasing and pouncing.

The urge to play

Most puppies will try to pick up almost anything they find lying around the house or garden. If the item has an unpleasant taste or causes pain he will probably abandon it. Everything else will either be played with and chewed, or presented for the owner's attention with a wagging tail and an expression that says 'please play'.

It is at this point that many owners inadvertently kill any inclination the dog may have had to give back the article to their hand. Instead he discovers either that he should never have anything in his mouth because the owner screams and shouts, or he should hang on for grim death and run like hell.

How to respond

The sensible reaction is to tell the puppy how clever he is, crouch down and encourage him to bring it to you so that you can gently take it from him. Obviously if every time he gives you his new things they are taken away and the game ends, he will soon stop allowing them to be taken. So do not just take the plaything away: instead always praise him for bringing it to you, rewarding him with a game with one of his own toys or a titbit. Regardless of how precious the item chosen as a plaything by the puppy, try to keep calm and do not fall into the trap of chasing him. You might succeed while he is young, but he will get wise to any tricks and will become more difficult to catch.

▲ If you find that your dog is about to pick up something inappropriate, by all means say 'no!', but then offer him an alternative.

MUST KNOW

No fight game
If the puppy has a tight grip on the article, do not let him turn this into a fight game as you try to remove the item from his jaws. If he sees another toy or titbit he will probably release his grip.

▶ Play retrieve exercise

'Play retrieve' is good fun and, once taught, great exercise for your dog when off the lead.

Chase the toy
Throw a toy that your dog likes a short distance, so that he automatically chases it.

It's a game

Until your dog can reliably come back when called, this game should always be taught on the lead. Use a special toy (as discussed on page 70) to keep the dog's interest in the retrieving. As he mouths the toy encourage him with 'good boy, fetch it!'.

Praise and encourage
Once he picks the toy up, walk back a few paces saying 'good dog, come' so he will bounce happily towards you.

Combine with 'sit'

It's easier to take the toy cleanly if your dog will 'sit' on request in front of you. Don't let him play tug. Gently take the article while telling him to leave it, and praise him as he gives it up.

Two-hand one-hand technique

You can also teach your dog that if you use both hands to take the article, one either side of his mouth, he must release it immediately, but if you use one hand only, it is an invitation to play tug.

want to know more?

Take it to the next level...

Go to...
▶ **Weekly training**– pages 74–141
▶ **Polishing off** – pages 142–151
▶ **Dog sports** – pages 160–177

Other sources
▶ **Your local pet store**
  great for stocking up on cheap and cheerful toys
▶ **Dog training classes**
  ask a friend who has dogs, check with your vet or look in the yellow pages
▶ **Internet**
  visit www.apdt.co.uk or www.traininglines.org.uk

weekly

training

Lots of short sessions with a successful conclusion each time will leave you and your dog looking forward to the next one. These sessions build up week-by-week to give you a solid ten-week training foundation course.

Weekly training programme

In this chapter we present our easy-to-follow dog training exercises. They build up on a week-by-week basis. If you follow and practise the exercises, step-by-step, then you and your dog should achieve a reasonable level of training by the end of the ten weeks.

No worries

The ten-week timescale presented here comes from our considerable experience of running dog training courses with many different breeds and ages of dogs. Do not worry if you feel you and your dog need more time on any particular aspect.

▶ The timing of praise and reward provide a fundamental platform for our training exercises. Do not get so hung up on trying to teach your dog that you forget the simple but necessary 'good boy'.

Consolidation

It is a vital part of our training philosophy that you consolidate each piece of an exercise before you move on. We have therefore broken down our exercises into stages to help you and your dog to develop them successfully. They are very basic and there is no great trick to them, but they should help you have a more socially acceptable and responsive companion. If your dog is having a problem, never be afraid to go back a step and revisit the basics.

Daily practice on the lead

All practice needs to be carried out with the dog on a collar and lead, even indoors. Ideally you should practise daily. Three or four ten-minute sessions are more beneficial than one long session. Start at a time and place where there are no distractions and you and your dog can concentrate.

As you join the stages together over the coming weeks, it is vitally important always to remember to praise your dog for each step correctly done, even if he needed help. The timing of the praise and reward is the most important part of any exercise. If the dog has sat well, but received the praise as he is getting up, he will think it is the getting up that is correct. Remember, you need a plan in your mind of what training you are going to do, as the dog has not got a clue.

Praise is all important

Also beware of simply concentrating so hard on teaching that you end up just telling the dog what to do, and then forgetting the all-important praise. Our training is not about teaching exercises for the sake of it, it is endeavouring to build a partnership that will make life more pleasant for you and your dog.

▶ Week One – Stand

The 'stand', 'sit' and 'down' positions can be usefully taught together as this helps your dog understand the difference between them.

The basic stand

Sit your dog at your left side. To put the dog in the stand, you should turn at a slight angle to face his side. Ensure the collar is loose and the lead already attached. Choose a quiet time and place preferably without distractions. You should encourage your dog to stay beside you and remain on the same spot.

Hind feet backwards

Hold the lead quite short in the right hand, over the dog's back and low along his spine, with the collar loose. As you give the 'stand' command, slide your left hand – with palm uppermost and thumb towards his hind leg – underneath the dog on the side nearest to you and move it towards his back leg. When your dog stands, praise him immediately. Your dog should stand by moving his hind feet backwards, not his front feet forwards.

Stop his back swinging out

If he attempts to move forwards check back along his spine with the lead, making sure the collar returns to being loose. If he attempts to swing his back end out away from you, slide your left hand all the way underneath and bring him back to the starting position.

Lead over the back

Remind him to 'stand' and praise him immediately with a 'good boy'. Repeated regularly the dog will soon learn. Then all you need to do is put the lead over his back, and as you slide your hand down and command, the dog should be standing. Praise him while you keep him standing still, and then release or move him to another position. Do not be in a hurry to move your left hand out from under the dog. Use it to tickle his tummy or just inside his hind leg. In every step do not forget the praise.

▶ Resist the urge to pick up your dog in a horseshoe fashion – otherwise 'stand' will simply mean to him 'mum's going to pick me up'. Make sure he is properly balanced.

▼ If your dog is very ticklish on the tummy, or unduly anxious, then you can pat the top of his head to praise him. You could also start with the dog against a wall; he will then be unable to swing away from you.

Week One – Sit

Many dogs learn to 'sit' on command easily, but they tend to want to face you. This can be very awkward if, for instance, your dog is on the lead and you are waiting on the pavement trying to cross the road, or you need to negotiate a park gate or climb over a stile.

The basic sit

In teaching this exercise you are not just teaching your dog to sit, you are teaching him to do it quickly and close to your left leg.

Dog at your left side

Start with your dog in the 'stand' position at your left side. Hold the lead quite short in your right hand, left hand at the dog's left side, thumb across his back, and fingers by his groin.

Left hand guiding

Command 'sit', and at the same time give a couple of checks up and back with the lead in your right hand while your left hand guides the dog into the 'sit' close by your left leg. His front feet should be level with yours. Make sure that the collar is loose but be ready to check again if necessary. Praise him immediately.

Keeping the correct sit position

Do not be in a hurry to move your left hand away as he may try to jump up. Praise him while he remains sitting still and then release or move him back into the 'stand'. You should always be ready to help him keep the correct position until you clearly indicate to him that he may move. Use your left hand to pat him low down on his flank, or your right hand to tickle his head and ears without losing control.

Ensuring the correct hand position

Try to make sure that your left hand is correctly positioned over your dog's back (as shown opposite). If you have a very bouncy and/or strong-willed dog, you may find initially that you are exerting a lot of pressure to keep him in the 'sit'. Try to get the praise in while he is sitting, even though he has no option but to remain sitting.

▲ If you are tempted to use the hand position shown above, you may be able to help your dog to sit, but you will not be able to guide him in close to your left leg.

▲ Initially this exercise may prove to be quite a struggle. Do persevere and don't give up until he relaxes. Remember to praise and keep calm.

Week One – Down

The 'down' is one of the most important exercises, if
not the most important, to teach your dog. If your dog is
running loose, even in a park or supposedly safe area,
dangers can still arise. Horses or children on bikes can
be hazardous around dogs. The 'down' is for safety.

Ensuring the essential position

Often you will not want to call your dog back to you as it could put
him in the line of danger. Left to his own devices your dog may
decide to chase after the horses or bikes and perhaps cause an
accident. If he will go 'down' instantly when told, even at a distance
from you, it could save his life.

Push with left hand
With your dog at your left side
standing still, give the 'down'
command. At the same time, move
the lead in the right hand from over
his spine down beside his right
shoulder, and with your left hand,
push down and diagonally back
towards the hind feet.

Hand over ridge

The middle finger and thumb of your left hand should be locked onto the ridge above his shoulders. Do not let your hand slip while making this movement, or you will find the dog sitting rather than going straight down – this is most likely to happen if you have a very smooth-coated dog, such as a Boxer.

Folding down

Your dog should 'fold' easily into the down position although you may need to apply quite steady pressure. Praise him as soon as he starts to go down. The right hand goes down with your dog, keeping the collar loose unless he attempts to resist; in this case a check down can be given.

From the stand

We prefer to teach a dog to go 'down' from the 'stand' position, simply because it is likely the dog will be standing or moving when you need to give the command. If he has to think about sitting first, he will go down too slowly and may move into the line of danger.

Stroke the back

Do not let him jump up straight away, praise him while he is still down, making sure the collar is loose. Stroke along the dog's back with your left hand, using light pressure that can be increased if he tries to move too soon. Wait until he is relaxed before you release him.

Moment of release

When he eventually relaxes, ease the tension on the lead, kneel down again and praise him while he is down. Now release him. Your dog can be taught to go back up into the 'sit' or 'stand' positions from the 'down'. However we consider it safer if the dog remains down until you release him.

Ending his game

Some dogs will try to turn this exercise into a game by nibbling or chewing at your hands or arms. A useful tip is to use your foot on the lead to free you arms. Quickly and quietly put your left foot on the lead very close to the collar and stand up. This removes your hands and arms from his mouth and effectively ends his game. When he relaxes, praise him verbally and lift the toe of your left foot to release the tension on the collar.

◀ Most puppies and young dogs will roll over onto their back or side, waving their feet in the air when placed in the 'down' position. This is quite natural – don't worry if your dog does this.

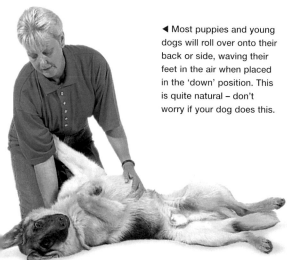

MUST KNOW

Tension

Be prepared to re-apply tension promptly should your dog try to jump up. However long it takes, do not finish the exercise while he is still struggling. Your dog should stay in 'down' until you release him. To develop this exercise, the dog must be still.

Week One – Watch

If you can get your dog's attention, when you want it, then he will be listening and ready for what comes next.

Learning to watch

The 'watch' command is a very useful tool in the training box. For example, if your dog has a grass seed near his eye and you need to remove it – if he will look at you and let you stroke his face, you can remove the seed with a minimal amount of hassle.

Correct watch
Get the dog to sit in front of you, hook your fingertips under the collar at the back of his neck. Command 'dog's name', 'watch' in a pleasant tone. At the same time slide your hands around the collar either side of the dog's neck up underneath the dog's muzzle.

Two-second eye contact
Stroke the sides of the dog's face with your thumbs, and praise him. If you get the dog to make eye contact for two or three seconds the first time, that will be sufficient. Now release him.

Making eye contact

The praise must be while you are making eye contact. Slowly build up the length of time that he will watch you, until all you need to do is give the command and he will look at you. Some dogs will hold the head position but avoid making eye contact. In this case try making squeaking noises and praise him instantly he looks, then release him.

Avoid tightening the grip

Be relaxed when doing this exercise. If you tighten your grip on his scruff or his collar, you will find yourself unable to stroke the sides of the dog's face when giving praise.

▲ Do not grip the dog by the scruff of his neck. Your dog may feel that he is going to be told off and start to struggle.

▲ Incorrect position: if you are standing with a larger dog your feet should be close to the dog's front feet. Bend your knees if necessary, but do not bend your back.

Watch – Small dog

The 'watch' command is important for small dogs as well as big dogs. However, if you have a little dog, you may have to teach this command slightly differently.

Use a pleasant tone

With a very small dog you might have to kneel with him between your knees. You should remember to keep your back as straight as possible – the aim is to encourage the dog to look up at you. Have your dog sit in front of you and hook your fingertips underneath the collar at the back of the dog's neck. Command 'dog's name' and 'watch' in a pleasant tone. At the same time slide your hands around the collar either side of the dog's neck up and underneath his muzzle and turn his head up encouraging him to make eye contact. In this position you should be able to stroke the sides of your dog's face with your thumbs, praising him at the same time. If you get your dog to make eye contact for two or three seconds the first time that is sufficient, then release him.

MUST KNOW

Calm measures

Remember to stroke the dog's face very slowly and calmly while using a gentle tone of voice because you don't want to get him over-excited.

Correct position

Eventually you will be able to command 'dog's name' and 'watch' and he will automatically look up to make eye contact with you. The principle and the end position are the same whether you have a small dog or a big dog, but your starting position is lower when you begin to teach this exercise to a small dog. Again, for those dogs that might hold the head position but avoid making eye contact, try making high squeaky noises to catch his eye and then praise the instant he looks. A food lure can also be very effective but make sure the dog remains sitting.

Eye level

If you have a bad back, and are unable to kneel, place the dog on a table or other raised surface.

▶ Leaning over like this is really only a good way to get back ache. Remember to try to keep your back straight, and go for eye contact, not nose contact.

Long down and long sit

The two exercises of 'long down' and 'long sit' are especially useful if you have a boisterous or strong-willed dog. They are designed to make the dog realize that you are dominant over him without losing your temper or perhaps resorting to physical violence, which never achieves anything.

Settling down

Don't practise these two exercises consecutively: do the 'long down' one day, and the 'long sit' the next. Pick the optimum time, both for yourself and the dog, particularly for the 'down'. Start when your dog is ready to settle of his own accord for a rest.

Into the 'down' position

With the collar and lead on the dog, put him in the 'down' position, making sure he is comfortable. Try to keep the dog 'down' for 30 minutes. If he is restless, a foot on the lead may be required. If the dog is anxious, occasional praise may be given.

Relaxing together
If your dog is relaxed then you can relax too. Try watching television or having a cup of tea, while keeping an eye on him.

When to release

Remember the aim is to get your dog in the 'long down' for half an hour. At the end of that time, if he is asleep, do not tiptoe off and leave him. Praise him while he is still 'down', then release. He may roll over and go back to sleep, and that is okay – you have made it clear to him that he has finished.

Don't make it a game

If your dog tries to make this a game by nibbling at your hands and arms, quickly slide your left foot up the lead, close to the collar and stand up. As he settles praise him and continue the exercise, releasing the tension as appropriate.

The long sit

The principle of getting the dog settled in the 'long sit' is exactly the same as for the 'long down' but it is only for 10 minutes.

Maintain the posture

As with the 'down', the position your dog is put in must be kept. If he moves put him back in the 'sit' position and start again. Try and ensure that the dog sits upright with his weight equally divided on both hips, not flopped to one side. At the end of the time, praise him while he is still sitting and then release him. If you prefer, you may stand up for this exercise.

Week Two – Fast down

The aim of this exercise is to put the dog in a 'down' position, as described in Week One, but to do it very quickly.

Into the 'down'
Take care to keep your left hand on his shoulder ridge and your right hand going down beside his shoulder. Praise him while he is 'down', keep him there for a count of five, then release him.

Walk in a circle
If your dog is starting to go down quite quickly because of the pressure of your hand, start to walk him in a left hand circle.

CHECKLIST

Week Two
• 'Stand'/ 'Sit'/ 'Down' Practise these exercises often.
• 'Watch' Try and increase the time the dog is making eye contact.
• 'Long sit' and 'long down' Alternate these exercises every other day.
• Remember to praise.

Right hand lead
Turn towards your dog, take the lead close to the clip with your right hand if it is not already there, and at the same time command 'down'.

Firm pressure

Give the 'down' command before you put your left hand on top of his shoulders, using firm pressure to help him go down very quickly. Do not let your hand slide down his back or down his neck, because this would allow him to sit or put his chin on the ground with his bottom in the air.

Fold into the down

With the correct pressure on his shoulders your dog should fold quickly, like a pack of cards. Remember to bring your right hand (which is holding the lead) down at the same time, so that you do not strangle him. Praise swiftly while he is down and then release.

Practise to drop on command

Do not put your hand on him before commanding; give him a second or two to do it himself, but do not wait too long and do not keep repeating the command. With practice he will realise that he should drop on the command before you touch him. This exercise should be repeated as often as possible. The more frequent the repetition, the faster the response will become.

▶ # Week Two – Down stay

If the dog has been going 'down' easily, has been praised while down, and is successfully completing 'long downs', this exercise should be straightforward.

Keeping still

Do not use your dog's name before the 'stay' command, as this may encourage him to move. 'Stay' to the dog, should mean 'you may relax, but do not change position or move from that spot, I will come back and release you'.

Keep an eye on him but do not stare. If you think that he is going to move, return immediately, even if you have not finished.

Settling your dog down
Place the dog in the 'down' as before, settling him so he is comfortable. If possible get him to roll on one hip as illustrated or, if he likes, flat on his side.

Lay down the lead
Using the lead on the long length, lay it on the ground to the right of the dog. Make sure the collar stays loose and that he does not get up.

Visual / verbal stay

Stand on the lead as close as possible to your dog; he should be settled, but if he is still trying to turn this into a game, you may need to keep tension on the lead until he has relaxed. Command 'stay' giving a visual command with the palm of your hand in front of his face. Hopefully he will not move and you will be able to praise him; alternatively you will be able to correct him quickly by re-apply the tension and reminding him to 'stay'.

Stand straight and count to five

Stand up straight beside him, count to five, then bend down and quietly 'praise' him, patting him gently. Then either use your release command and let your dog get up, or command 'stay' and repeat the exercise.

MUST KNOW

Let him know

Do not be too exuberant with your praise as you want your dog to remain calmly down; but he needs to know that he is doing the exercise correctly and that you are pleased with him.

A pace away on the lead

Once your dog has got used to you bending over him and saying 'stay' and then you standing up, try taking a pace or two away from him (assuming he is very settled).

Move to the right

Move away to the right along the line of the lead so that you have control and he cannot get away from you. Keep an eye on him all the time so that you can forestall any attempt on his part to move.

Stand upright

Stand upright, keeping an eye on your dog and count to five. If he looks like he is going to move, get back to him straight away, even if you have not yet counted to five.

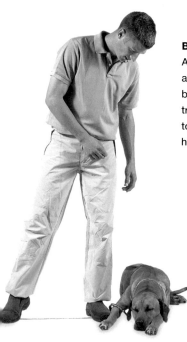

Back along the line

After you have counted to five, return to the dog along the line of the lead. Stay upright, do not bend down at this stage as he is more likely to try and get up to greet you if you bend. Try not to talk to the dog unless you have to correct him. Praise comes fractionally later.

Count before releasing him

Stand upright beside him, but do not allow him to get up while you count to two. If he starts to get up, try and use tension with your foot on the lead to prevent it. The reason for counting to two before you praise him is that if you fuss him immediately upon your return, he is more likely to want to get up to meet you in anticipation that the exercise has ended.

Bend down and praise

After you have counted to two, bend down and praise him, making sure he stays in the 'down' position. (If you fuss him too soon, he is more likely to get up to meet you.) It doesn't matter if he rolls on his back while receiving the praise. Release him or settle him and repeat the exercise.

Week Three – Stand

Out of the three positions, 'stand' can be the most difficult for a dog to learn. Standing on four feet is not a problem, standing still is, or can be! Always be ready to help him up and do not forget to make sure that he is balanced.

Standing still

You are now trying to get your dog to stand still for longer periods (as opposed to just getting him up into the stand position).

Do not attempt to move your hands away until he is absolutely steady. This is an exercise which can be worked on while you are grooming the dog or if he is in the vet's for an examination or check up.

CHECKLIST

Week Three
• 'Stand'/'Sit'/'Down' Practise often.
• 'Watch' Continue to increase the time that the dog makes eye contact. Remember to praise while your dog is making eye contact, not after.
• 'Long sit' and 'long down' Alternate these exercises every other day.
• 'Fast down' Practise as in Week Two.
• 'Down stay' Practise as in Week Two.

Left hand position
With your dog settled in the stand, keep your left hand under the tummy for a bitch, while with a male tickle just inside the hind leg. Lay the lead over the dog's back with your right hand as illustrated (with a small dog, lay the lead down on the ground).

Lead over back like a saddle

Place the lead over the dog's back like a saddle so that it does not slip and distract him. Do not try to lie the lead along the length of the dog's spine. Remind him to stand, drop your left hand away and stand upright and count to five. He should be keeping all four feet still. If he starts to fidget, pick up the lead, put your left hand back and remind him to stand before trying again.

Left hand to dog's tummy

After you have counted to five, put your left hand back under his tummy, while your right hand goes to pick up the lead. Praise him quietly while he is standing still and then release him or ask him to go into the 'sit' or 'down'.

WEEKLY TRAINING

Week Three – Side watch

Now that your dog is watching you from the front, you can begin to teach the 'watch' from the side. The main use for this exercise is at the start of heelwork.

Concentration

If your dog is watching you then hopefully he is also paying attention and is less likely to be distracted by his surroundings.

In the same manner as teaching the 'watch' from the front, use a pleasant tone in your commands. Make sure you are not nagging. Most importantly, get the praise in while the dog is making eye contact, not as he looks away. Build the time up, using literally seconds at a time, as your dog's ability to concentrate increases.

With a large dog

Your dog should be in the sit at your left side with the lead held in your right hand. Move your left hand over the top of the dog's head and slide it down so the fingertips are under the dog's jaw. Command 'dog's name' and 'watch' in a pleasant tone, while turning his head up against your body to make eye contact. Praise him as he does this, then release him or repeat the step.

With a small dog

The principle is the same with a small dog, but obviously you will need to bend lower. Try to bend sideways, sliding your left hand down your left leg rather than leaning forward to obstruct the dog's view.

MUST KNOW

Ending the exercise

If you are not moving off into heelwork, finish this exercise by using your release command, taking a pace backwards so your dog turns towards you for a fuss.

With experience

Practised enough, you should eventually be able to command 'dog's name' and 'watch' and have him turn his head up to make eye contact with you. When teaching this exercise, it can be useful to exaggerate the upward tilt of the head to help the dog understand what is required. Once your dog has learnt the exercise the tilt may not be so marked, but the eyes will still make contact.

▶ Week Three – Heelwork

You must teach heelwork with a slack lead and loose collar.
Your dog cannot learn if the lead is tight. While you may be
able to keep him by your side with physical strength, this will
not teach him anything.

Feeling

Some dogs are very good at not quite pulling but still
keeping the lead just taut; they can feel where their
owner is and so do not have to look or listen.

Dog on your left side
Have your dog in the 'sit' at your left side watching you.
As he sits and watches you, praise each action.
Allow 10–15cm (4–6in) of slack lead.

Stepping off on the left
The lead will probably have been in
your right hand as you helped the
dog 'sit' and 'watch'. Just before
stepping off transfer it to your left
hand. Command dog's name and
'heel' and step off smartly with the
left leg, and praise immediately.

Lead in left hand
Ideally, hold the lead in
your left hand only and
position your hand in
front of your left leg. If
you find this difficult,
try hooking your thumb
into your trouser
pocket to achieve the
correct position.

Using both hands

With a particularly strong dog you may need to hold the lead in both hands. Remember, keep the collar loose on your dog's neck. Think of the lead as a teaching aid, not as a tow rope for the dog to pull.

Six to ten paces

Step off in a positive manner. Praise the dog immediately. Do not wait for him or check him forward. If he does not move quickly with you, he will check himself. Walk in a left hand circle at a brisk pace, aiming for six to ten paces with the dog in the correct position. Praise him all the time and remind him to 'heel'.

Take a step back

Now release the dog after successfully completing a couple of paces by taking a few steps backward. Use your dog's name so that he turns and comes in to you for the praise. Keep it fun; intersperse short bursts of correct heelwork with time out for a quick game.

Do not say anything

If, at some stage, the dog moves out of the correct heelwork position by pulling forwards or sideways do not say anything. The lead is going to tell the dog that he is not doing what you want.

Move hand to lead

You must move your hand towards the dog wherever it is, to give more slack in the lead. Don't let the lead lengthen out as it will still be tight. You can't check on a tight lead, you can only pull.

MUST KNOW

Checking

The check has to be strong enough for the size of dog or his sensitivity. A large, sensitive dog may only need a slight check, a small, stubborn dog might require a firmer check.

Firm check

Check in the opposite direction to that which your dog is moving. The check should be firm enough to get him back in the correct position by your left leg with a loose collar – so you can praise him.

Repeat check

Check as often as necessary. Remember not to speak as you check. It is more important to get the praise in as the dog returns to your side. Hopefully he will look at you as you praise him. Then you can remind him, 'heel'.

Rewarding your dog

If your dog is walking nicely to heel, do not be afraid to give him the occasional pat. Preferably use your right hand because moving your left hand may push him away from you. Talk to him if he is paying attention to you, so that he knows you are pleased with him. If you are using food as a reward, the occasional treat produced from your right hand pocket will reinforce this.

Week Four – Heel and sit

While you may know you are going to stop, your dog has no idea, so it is vital you do not do so suddenly.

No sudden halts

If you stop abruptly your dog will be taken by surprise and will be at the length of the lead in front of you. He will be checked unnecessarily for something that is not his fault.

Transfer the lead
While moving with your dog, transfer the lead to the right hand in preparation for halting.

CHECK LIST

Week Four
• 'Stand' as in the previous week, but increase the count to ten or twelve.
• 'Sit' Practise as often as you can.
• 'Down' Practise as often as you can.
• 'Watch' Practise at the front and side. Aim for longer periods of attention.
• 'Long sit' and 'long down' If your dog is still unsettled alternate every other day.
• 'Fast down' Continue left hand circles, helping your dog to go down quickly.
• 'Down stay' Continue as in Week Three but move three paces forward off the lead and count to ten. Stand sideways on to your dog, don't face him directly.
• 'Heelwork' Left hand circles only – aim to get him to stay at your left side on a slack lead.

Hand close to the trigger hook

You must try and get your hand as near to the trigger hook as possible as this will help you control where the dog sits. This may be more difficult with a small dog, but it is important because it helps you keep him close and makes it easier to help him into the correct sit position.

Left hand helps into sit

Command 'sit' and use your left hand to help your dog into the sit as you stop (as you have already practised in the stationary position). Praise your dog while he is sitting and encourage him to 'watch'. Then either continue heelwork or release him.

Sit in heelwork – Big dog

This exercise is the same whether the dog is small or large.
However it is a lot easier if you have a big dog as you do
not need to bend so far to reach the clip on the lead.

Preparation

It is even more important to get your hand close to the clip
in order to control a big dog. He could pull you completely
off balance if you stop suddenly, and you will find it difficult
to get him sitting close to your left leg.

Heelwork position
With the lead in the left hand, this is the correct position
for heelwork. Note the dog watches the handler; this is
the ideal response.

Preparing to sit
Resist the temptation to bend over your
dog. Instead, try and stay as upright as
possible. Bend your knees if necessary,
while your right hand is checking up and
slightly back and your left hand is ready
to help him into the 'sit'. Thumb over the
dog's back and fingers flat against his
groin as illustrated.

Stay balanced

The command 'sit' should be given as you stop. It is important to make sure that you are balanced, probably with feet slightly apart, so that you do not fall over your dog as you put him in the sit. Then use your left hand to guide him to sit close to your left leg. Remember to keep your thumb over his back and your fingers flat against him, not digging into him. His front feet should be level with your feet and facing the same direction.

Avoid any leaping up

Praise your dog as he sits, and do not let him leap up – you may need to keep your left hand in position while you praise him. If he is leaning on your left leg that is quite okay. Then either release or ask him to 'watch' and continue heelwork.

MUST KNOW

Praise in the sit

Don't forget to praise your dog with a 'good dog' the moment he sits, even though you have helped him into this position.

▶ Week Four – Sit stay

Your dog must be steady in the 'sit' position before you attempt the 'sit stay'. If he is not steady when you are standing next to him, he certainly will not let you take a pace away.

Calming your dog's worries

Some dogs initially worry when their owner disappears for a second behind them and tend to leap up. If this habit is persistent with your dog, you should do a half circle in front of the dog, walking backwards to the starting point. The arc can be gradually increased until it is a full circle – do not rush this.

It is very important that you praise your dog gently and calmly: being exuberant in your praise is likely to make your dog move.

Dog on left with long lead
Start with your dog at the left side in the 'sit' position. The lead should be at the long length, not clipped up short.

Right hand signal
Command 'stay' in a pleasant but firm tone. At the same time use your right hand to give a visual command with the palm of your hand in front of your dog's face.

Correct grip on lead

Take the end of the lead in your right hand. With the flat of your left hand, palm uppermost, take up the slack in the lead over the dog's head. Keep the lead straight and do not allow it to loop around his head.

Hand not too high

Do not have your hand too high up in the air, as you will be unable to correct the dog if he moves, but do make sure the collar is loose. Step one pace to the right.

Circling your dog

If your dog is steady, move slowly forward and around the dog in a circle. Remind him 'good dog', 'stay', if necessary, in a pleasant tone of voice.

Check upwards

If he moves, or starts to fidget, check upwards with the left hand and remind him to 'sit stay', and praise if he does. Try to correct at arm's length rather than going right back to him. Do not use his name because by doing so he may be distracted and get up. Just use 'good boy, sit stay'.

Your dog should be aware of the meaning of the word 'sit' by now, but is learning 'stay' in this exercise. Eventually you will be able to drop 'sit' and just use 'stay'.

Watch on the move

Keep your eye on the dog all the time you are moving. It is better to remind him to 'sit stay' and praise gently rather than letting him move and then correcting him.

Keeping the right pace

Use a nice steady pace; do not rush or the dog may startle, and do not go too slowly or he may think you are teasing. As you get back level with your dog's right shoulder take a step to the left so you are close beside him where you started.

Count to two

Stand by his side, count to two and then praise him gently without letting him move. Some dogs will try and slide into the 'down'. Be ready to check and remind him to 'sit', try not to let him spoil the exercise by making a mistake at the end of it. Then either repeat or release him.

▶ Week Five – Fast down

You now need to start building up the distance between you and your dog, while not allowing him to ignore your instructions. Ideally you need a friend or family member to get you started.

Get someone to help

Having found someone to help you, give the lead to them and have them walk the dog away from you – no more than 2m (6.5ft). Your friend is there to stop the dog coming forward and, if necessary, help your dog go 'down'. Your helper should not speak to the dog.

CHECK LIST

Week Five
• 'Stand' As before, if the dog is steady command 'stand' stepping off with the right foot. Move two paces in front. Turn and go straight back to his side, keep him standing still while praising gently, then repeat or release.
• 'Sit' Practise often.
• 'Down' Practise.
• 'Watch' Practise at front and side aiming for longer periods of attention.
• 'Long sit' and 'long down' Continue if you have a very strong-willed or bouncy dog.
• 'Down stay' Put the dog in the down, lay the lead on the ground stretched out to the right. Command 'down', 'stay'. Take one pace to the right along the lead and then five paces forward. Stand sideways to him, count to 15 and return.
• 'Heelwork' Use left-hand circles. Include quick 'sits' at the halt.

Command down
As dog and helper turn to face you command 'down'. Do not say his name and try not to bend as this will encourage the dog to come towards you. If necessary, clap your hands or stamp your foot to get your dog's attention. This should only be done when you are first attempting this exercise to give the dog every opportunity to succeed.

Hand signal is fine
Using a hand signal is acceptable so long as you do not bend. Some people prefer to use a hand-up-in-the-air signal, which they feel will be seen better from a distance, but most people automatically point down as they command.

Helping hand

If he does not go down, repeat the command 'down'. The person holding the lead should use their left hand on the dog's shoulder to put your dog into the 'down'.

Focused dog

Tell him 'good boy, stay down' and get back to him quickly and quietly. Your friend should make sure the dog does not get up, avoiding fussing and eye contact with him, so as to keep your dog's attention focused on you.

No overbending

You should return in an upright stance as any premature bending almost certainly will encourage the dog to try and leap up. When reaching the dog you should go down to him to praise him.

Praise and pat

Your friend/helper should not be involved in fussing the dog. You must make sure that the dog receives his praise and patting while still in the 'down' position. When you are ready you can release the dog. This exercise should be repeated frequently. If the dog is responding well in a quiet situation then it can be practised when there are distractions.

Week Five – Sit stay

Your dog should be quite relaxed and steady while you are circling around him slowly. If not more work needs to be done on that basic part of the exercise.

Initial sit and praise

Always remember to praise him for the parts done correctly; this includes the initial 'sit' before attempting a clear 'stay' command, As with the 'down stay' do not use the dog's name as this is likely to make him move. The praise must be given calmly, that is not overexcitedly but enough to let the dog know you are pleased with him.

A small pace to the right
Command 'stay'. Take a small pace to the right and then return immediately to his side. Count to two before praising him quietly and then remind him to 'stay'.

To the end of the lead
This time move out to the right to the end of the lead and then return immediately. Keep a nice steady confident speed, and do not move too quickly nor too slowly. Praise the dog quietly as before and remind him to 'stay'.

Small step to the right

Next, take a small step to the right and walk out in front of the dog to the end of the lead. Keep an eye on your dog all the time in case he thinks about moving. If you suspect that he is going to move, try to get back to his side to prevent him moving prematurely and breaking the exercise.

Back to dog's side

Do not stand and stare at the dog but return immediately to the dog's side, praising as previously described. Always remember to praise your dog for the parts that are done correctly. This includes the initial sit before attempting a clear 'stay' command. Then either repeat the exercise or release the dog.

▶ Week Five – Present

The front present exercise is part of teaching your dog to come instantly when called, in a controlled manner. The emphasis should be on the command 'come' and the praise.

Straight ahead

Walk in a straight line with the dog at heel; ideally the lead should be held in the left hand ready for the next step. Do not allow the lead to lengthen by sliding through your hand. The length of your arm and the length of lead between your hand and the dog's neck is sufficient for this exercise.

Back step

Tell your dog what you are going to do by calling his name and commanding 'come'. Bend slightly and extend your arm. Check with the lead and walk backwards on the same line at a steady pace; do not attempt to run.

Lead under chin

Praise your dog with 'good boy, come' as he turns to face you, and keep the lead low so that it is under his chin. Do not try and push your dog forcibly away from you – step back away from him and he will have to turn toward you. If he's a big dog, try tickling his nose as he comes in.

Hands as targets

Praise your dog and remind him to 'come' as you continue to move back another few paces; his attention should be totally focused on you. Keep your hands together low down – these should be the target your dog is coming towards.

Encourage him towards you

Make sure the lead and collar are loose. If your dog attempts to go past you, check and encourage him to come straight in front. Use your voice to keep the dog's attention and making eye contact will certainly help in this exercise. Remember, the dog is being encouraged in; he is not being reeled in like a fish on the end of a line.

MUST KNOW

From on- to off-lead

In order for your dog to develop a reliable habit off-lead of coming in close when called, it is essential that the praise at this stage be enthusiastic and genuine and that the lead and collar remain loose. This exercise can be practised any time the dog is on the lead and preferably when he is distracted, for example, when he is watching other dogs or joggers. It does not have to be set up as a formal exercise. Frequent repetitions of this exercise at random intervals are enormously beneficial. Your dog should not be off-lead if he cannot be trusted to return to you when called, whatever the distraction.

Coming in straight

To help your dog come in straight you may find it useful to walk backwards with your feet slightly apart so that the dog is not treading on your toes. Once he is coming in straight, you can prepare to stop.

Nose to hand

Viewed from the side, note that the dog is pushing his nose into his owner's hands, the collar and lead are loose and low under his chin. With a small dog, his nose will obviously not be in your hands, so use your voice to encourage him to look up to your face or hands.

Hand under the chin

As you stop, make sure you are balanced, especially with a big dog who may knock you over. Just before you stop, grip your dog's collar under his chin with your left hand, to help guide him in and keep his head up. Use your fingertips under the collar as shown here. Do not worry about the lead, it can stay in the same hand, or you can let it drop once you have hold of the collar.

MUST KNOW

Small dog

Make sure you keep the lead under the dog's chin even with a small dog. This is important because it helps you keep control of where the dog sits.

Bring head up

Keeping your grip on his collar under his chin with your left hand, bring your dog's head up as you command 'sit'. At the same time use your right hand on his bottom to help him sit close in front. Try to do this smoothly in an all-in-one movement without grabbing and pushing the dog around.

Reinforce the reward

Once your dog is sitting in front of you, ask him to 'watch'. Praise him warmly. If you are occasionally using a titbit or toy to reinforce the reward, now is a good time to produce it from your pocket. Toys and titbits should be an added bonus that the dog hopes he will get but does not always receive. This usually helps keep him interested and happy to return to his owner.

Week Six – About turn

When you change direction in heelwork you must let your dog know.

Body posture

For the 'about turn' you turn to the right and use the dog's name in a pleasant tone, as if you were calling him. This should encourage him to look up at you and help him come round. Remember to look in the direction you are going as this alters your body posture, giving the dog a clear signal of the change of direction. You might try practising this to begin with using a line on an empty car park or tennis court.

Don't look down
Use your dog's name and slow down slightly, but do not look down at the dog as this will tend to push him back.

Slide your left hand across
Turn your head to look the way you want to go and slide your left hand across your body to the right, not up. Aim to reach as far as your right hand trouser or skirt pocket (see left). This will take up the slack in the lead so your dog stays close as he turns (see right). Remember to praise.

DOG

HANDLER

Stay on the line

Once you are out of the turn, replace your left hand to your normal heelwork position and return to normal walking pace. Two points to remember: your left hand should remain in contact with your body as you make the turn and you must try and return on the same line as you walked up, not in a horseshoe shape.

CHECK LIST

Week Six

• 'Stand' As before, if your dog is steady command 'stand', step off with the right foot, and move four paces in front of your dog. Turn sideways onto him, count to five and then go back to his side. Keep him standing still, praising gently, then release.

• 'Sit' and 'down' Practise as often as you can.

• 'Watch' Increase the period of attention.

• 'Long sit' and 'long down' Continue as needed.

• 'Down stay' As before but now take ten paces forward and then count to 15 before returning to your dog.

• 'Sit stay' With your dog in the sit position at your left hand side, command 'stay' and place the lead on the floor. Move one pace to the right and two paces to the front, count to five and return to your dog.

Week Six – Fast down

By now your dog should be going down instantly when told, so this is the time to practise the exercise outside with some distractions. If you have someone to help, proceed with the exercise as described in Week Five.

Use the lead
If you do not have a helper, tie your dog up on a long lead, making sure it is tied low down. You should be concentrating on the 'down' at a distance, not the 'stand', so try to settle the dog quickly in the 'stand' and walk away. Just the fact that you have walked away will usually keep the dog's attention and position, especially if you keep telling him 'good dog, stand'. You may need to tie two leads if one is not long enough.

Command stand
Do not be tempted to try this with the dog off the lead, because if he refuses, you may be unable to enforce it and he will learn that he can ignore you. Command the dog to 'stand' and position the lead as you have been doing in the 'stand' exercise. Now step off with the right foot.

Take six paces

Walk about six paces out in front of your dog and turn to face him. Command 'down', remembering not to use his name as this will encourage him to move forward. If at any stage he does not go down instantly, you should return promptly to him and insist.

Get back

When he goes down praise him, tell him 'stay' and get back to him. If he gets up as you are returning, stand still and command him 'down' again and continue.

Praise on the down

Praise him, keeping him in the 'down' until you are ready. Then give your release command and let him up.

▶ Week Seven – Fast down

Your dog should go 'down' instantly when told, even faster now. You should still be working on building up distance, but the stand should be improving as well. If no one can assist, repeat the exercise as in Week Six.

In the 'stand'
Place your dog in the 'stand'. Pass the lead back to your assistant. Your helper must not distract your dog, but can help by holding one hand under the tummy as well as making sure the collar stays loose.

Hand signals
Remind your dog to 'stand', using your right hand to give a signal, while your left hand can stay under his tummy until the last moment.

CHECK LIST

Week Seven
• 'Watch' Build up the time at front and side.
• 'Down stay' Go to the down, remove the lead putting it away in your pocket. Say 'stay', take a small pace to the right, ten paces forward and count to 15. Return to your dog, clipping your lead on while he is still down. Praise him and then release.
• 'Sit stay' From the 'sit' at the left hand side, remove the lead and put in pocket. Command 'stay', take a pace to the right and two paces to the front. Turn sideways on to the dog, count to five and return to him. Make sure the dog remains in the 'sit' while you praise him and clip his lead on, then release.

WEEKLY TRAINING

Dog's attention on you
Step off with your right foot, keeping an eye on your dog as you move. The dog's attention should be focused on you, not on the assistant.

Keeping your dog standing
Your helper may also gently put her left hand under the dog's tummy to keep your dog standing if he has started to anticipate the exercise and tries to go down too soon. If he does anticipate – do not tell him off. Quietly reposition and try again with the aid of the helper. Walk out in front of the dog, turn to face him and command 'down'. Remember to increase the distance over the course of the week.

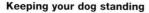

Down fast
He should go down immediately. Tell him 'good dog, stay', and get back to him. If he does not go down, the assistant should help him. Remember to praise him while he is still down before releasing him.

Right turn in heelwork

You should still be practising straight lines and about turns with sits at the start and finish most of the time. Sometimes just release your dog by calling his name and taking a pace backwards as when you started 'heelwork' in Week Three.

Right angle

Practise left and right hand circles, also incorporating 'front presents'. Rather than doing circles all the time, you should now be seeking to teach your dog to do a proper right angle turn. The 'right turn' is executed in much the same way as the 'about turn'.

Slow up slightly

Slow up very slightly so that you give your dog enough time to come round with you, especially if you have a small dog. It can help to use slightly smaller steps rather than large ones, to help your dog keep the correct heelwork position.

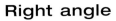

Look and slide the hand

Turning your head to look the way you want to go, call your dog's name in a pleasant tone, and slide your left hand across your body to the right to take up the slack in the lead. Make sure you keep your hand in contact with your body and that your hand slides across your body, not upwards. Remember to praise your dog.

Left hand position

As you come out of the turn, replace your left hand to your normal heelwork position and return to a normal pace, praising your dog and reminding him to 'heel'.

Wait for recall

Only if the 'sit stay' is reliable should you start this exercise. If the 'sit stay' isn't steady then continue with 'front presents' incorporated in heelwork.

Avoiding confusion

Never practise this exercise immediately before or after a 'sit stay' because it will cause the dog to become confused and you will almost certainly lose your 'sit stay'.

Now we are going to try and make this exercise as different to a 'sit stay' as possible. We are only going to use 'sit' as the command because we are going to ask the dog to move. Do not use your dog's name until then. Concentrate on praising quietly and calmly while reminding him to 'sit'.

Sit at left hand side
Your dog should be put in the 'sit' position at the left hand side. Make sure that he is settled and preferably not flopped on one hip.

Lengthen the lead
Unclip the lead onto the long length, making sure that the collar stays loose and your dog does not move out of the 'sit'.

Lead in left hand

Hold all of the lead in the left hand, praising the dog and reminding him to 'sit'. Remember not to use his name as you do not want him to move until you are ready.

Move close in

Using a hand signal with the verbal command, start to move close in front of your dog.

Face your dog

Facing your dog, remind him to 'sit'. Keeping a loose lead, hold the dog's attention by saying 'good dog, sit' in a firm but pleasant tone – remember not to use his name.

Slowly back off

Start to move confidently backwards, to the end of the lead. Maintaining the hand signal may help keep your dog sitting. As you pay the lead out smoothly, ensure your dog's collar stays loose, with no tension on the lead.

Move steadily

Move at a steady pace, not too fast nor too slow as if teasing, keeping his attention by continually telling him 'good dog, sit'. If your dog looks like he is going to move, then go straight back to settle him.

Count to two

When you get to the end of the lead, stand still and count to two. The dog's attention should still be focused on you. Your flat palm signal is reinforcing the command.

End of the lead

Bend slightly, extending the arm with the lead in preparation for checking and calling, and drop your other hand. If your dog tries to anticipate the recall because you have moved, remind him 'sit' and go back to him and start again.

Check to the lead

As you command 'dog's name', 'come', give a check to the lead, which should be sufficient to make the dog move immediately.

MUST KNOW

Remember
To stop him anticipating the recall, each time you call your dog out of the 'sit' position, do three versions where you keep him sitting and return to him instead.

Praise
As soon as he starts to get up to come to you praise him. Make sure you let him know how pleased you are with him.

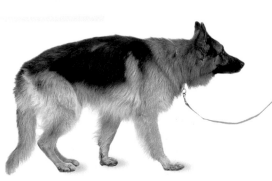

Right hand help
Left hand in the collar, as in 'front present' (see page 124) and use your right hand to help him into the 'sit' in front of you.

Praise repeated
Praise him while he is sitting and watching, and then repeat the first part of the exercise, but instead of calling your dog out of the 'sit' position you return to him; praise him for sitting still. This will stop him anticipating that he will always be called out of the 'sit'.

Return to his side
Turn to stand back by his side, praising again before releasing.

Week Eight – Left turn

To do a right-angle left turn in heelwork, your dog needs to stop momentarily as you make the turn.

Head and shoulders

When making the left turn, the speed will vary depending on the size of dog you have. But his head and shoulder should stay by your left leg.

CHECK LIST

Week Eight
• 'Stand' Increase to eight paces and count to ten.
• 'Watch' Practise front and side positions. He should respond to the word 'watch'.
• 'Long sit' and 'long down' Continue as necessary.
• 'Fast down' Walk out 12 paces in front of the dog.
• 'Down stay' Increase to 30 seconds away from dog.
• 'Sit stay' Take five paces to the front and count to ten.
• 'Recall' Don't attempt this off the lead. If he gets away from you all the hard work will be undone. Try a longer lead.
• 'Heelwork' Practise heelwork with the 'sit' at the start and halt, including about turns, right turns and front presents.

Back to start
Then return to a normal pace. Some sensitive dogs may over-react initially, so keep their confidence with praise.

Smooth start
Try to make your hand movement as smooth as possible as your dog should not need to be checked.

Left hand position
Praise your dog and replace your left hand to the normal heelwork position as you step out of the turn.

Back
At the same time command 'back'; turn your head in the direction you want to go and execute the turn.

Re-position the lead
Slide the lead round behind your back with your left hand, keeping it in contact with your body. This stops your dog from moving forward.

want to know more?

Take it to the next level...

Go to...
▶ Polishing off – pages 142–151
▶ Using rewards – pages 152–159
▶ Dog essentials – pages 178–181

Other sources
▶ Dog training classes
  ask a friend who has trained their dog; or try your local vet, local library and local pet food supplier. The local yellow pages can also start you off
▶ Local dog kennels
  a very good place to seek first-hand advice about dogs and training courses
▶ Internet
  visit www.the-kennel-club.org.uk

polishing

off

Having completed the first eight weeks of the course on home ground, it is time to venture further afield for the final two weeks and work towards a good response in new environments.

Outdoor training

By now you should have noticed an improvement in your dog's behaviour that you should aim to maintain during the final two weeks of the training course. The extent of the improvement will depend on the variables mentioned at the start of the book.

CHECK LIST

Weeks Nine & Ten
- 'Stand' Increase to 15 paces away, and count to ten.
- 'Sit', 'down', 'watch' Continue practising.
- 'Fast down' If steady in the 'stand' remove the lead, proceed as in Week Seven. If he moves forward, go back to having a friend hold the lead, or tie the dog up.
- 'Down stay' Increase to one minute away from your dog.
- 'Heelwork' As in Week Eight, but now adding 'left turns.'
- 'Sit stay' As in Week Seven, but take ten paces to the front, increase to ½ minute away from the dog.
- 'Recall' Try a long line instead of a lead.

Expectations

Your dog should at least be doing all the exercises at home in a quiet environment with no distractions – if not he needs considerably more time and effort spent on him.

Be honest with yourself: have you really practised as often as you should have? If the answer is no, then you know what to do. If the answer is yes, then perhaps you have either a slow-thinking dog so be patient, or a more dominant dog, so be consistently firm.

Venturing outside

If he is doing the exercises nicely at home then you can reasonably expect a good response elsewhere. Do not make excuses or give repeat commands if he does not respond promptly.

▶ This well-behaved dog is sitting under control with three distractions at once – food, something to chase and a pond.

POLISHING OFF

Help him get it right so that you can praise him. Always expect him to be distracted in new surroundings and be prepared to enforce each command, then you can be pleasantly surprised if he does it correctly first time and you will be ready to praise him. Your dog should have a good grasp of all the basic exercises by Week Ten – 'stand', 'sit' and 'down', 'watch', 'long sit' and 'long down', 'fast down', 'down stay ', 'heelwork', 'sit stay' and 'recall'.

▲ No one likes unruly dogs in a park – especially picnickers. This well-behaved dog is walking past on a loose lead while the picnickers' dog practises his 'long down'.

Be prepared to help

Don't be surprised if your dog does not respond as reliably in a strange place, or with unusual distractions. Do not lose your temper and always be prepared to go back to the first steps if there is a problem.

As before, do not make excuses, and do not give repeat commands if he does not respond promptly. The key is to help him get it right so that you can praise him, and the greater variety of surroundings you can practise in, the more dependable he will become.

Everyday routine should include exercises based on training for your dog.

▲ Dogs should always be kept under control around livestock. This dog is a good example of sitting quietly with a loose lead despite the curious cows.

▼ Outdoors there are plenty of opportunities to work with distractions. In reality training is never finished.

Everyday exercises

Make every effort to find opportunities for using your training exercises in your daily life with your dog. For example, you can use 'stand' when grooming your dog, drying his feet after a walk, or to check him over for grass seeds in the summer, not to mention when you take him to the vet. 'Watch' can be used as his face is examined. 'Sit' or 'down' can be practised at dinner time, when you put his lead and collar on, going in and out of the car, or to stop him pushing first through doorways.

Training should be fun

As we have stressed throughout, training should be fun for you and your dog. It should be possible to incorporate training sessions in your daily outings with your dog. They do not have to be formal sessions as such. So making the dog 'sit' before he is told to jump in the car for a ride to the supermarket or park can be used as a training exercise. The ride is part of the reward for most dogs.

Continuing to incorporate training with everyday activities; do not just let him leap out to run riot when you get to the park. He should 'sit' or 'down' until you tell him that he may get out. Indeed it would not hurt to ask for a few minutes of obedience before starting your walk.

POLISHING OFF

146

▲ Although this dog is off the lead, the value of the owner's special toy and attention outweigh the attraction of the other dogs.

Stopping with the dog in the 'sit' at every kerb emphasizes that you are leading, and the dog can be rewarded with a titbit as well as a word of praise, and then continued movement, which is a reward in itself for most dogs. Just because your dog does an exercise correctly once, it does not mean that he has learned that exercise.

So keep using your training aids and never take unnecessary chances, however well-trained you feel he is.

Think safety

While the training intensity may diminish, the practice should be on-going.

Always think safety first. Accidents happen, doors get left open for example, so if he will go down instantly on 'fast down', it could save his life. 'Sit stay' and 'down stay' can be used when you do not want him moving around, for whatever reason. However well trained you think your dog is, under unexpected circumstances, such as a cat suddenly appearing, he can forget his training and learned behaviour and revert to instinctive behaviour.

Problems with recall

Perhaps the most common problem we encounter is the dog that will not come back when called. Our training exercises are designed to troubleshoot this problem, but some dogs still need further work.

When more work is needed

Hopefully you will have followed our advice already in this book, by not standing and continually shouting your dog's name and 'come', when it cannot be enforced. All this does is contradict the on-lead training and show your dog that he does not have to come instantly. There is no doubt that some dogs need a lot more work on the 'recall' command than others. They need a lot more work on increasingly long leads or lines recalling them from various distractions. Remember to give enthusiastic praise and reinforce this with a titbit or a game with a toy.

▼ Some pet dogs and cats (like this pair) get along fine, but if your dog is a cat chaser, keep him on a line in the house for a while. Make sure the line does not have a handle that could snag, and that the line is long enough to be caught easily if the dog tries to chase.

◄ Holding the end of the lead close in front of her body, the handler walks off without giving any warning to the dog.

Using a long line

Long-line work helps to get your dog to pay attention, instead of responding to checks on the lead. This is essential in recalls and heelwork. Work in a square pattern, the number of steps depending on space available and size of dog. Ten to 12 paces is ample. Grip the end of the line securely in front of the body with both hands, then step off without any warning or commands and take the steps before making a sharp right turn and stopping. Taken unawares the dog checks himself at the end of the line. Ignore the dog, counting silently to 20 before stepping off and repeating the exercise. This may need many repetitions but the dog will realize that he needs to pay attention to you. Then heel commands and praise can be introduced.

▲ Her sudden halt has caught the dog unawares and he looks to see what she is doing.

► With practice the dog now pays more attention to the handler so that he is not caught out again.

Taking it further

Even if you are happy with the standard of dog control after the training course, this isn't the time to stop the exercises. There are usually problems to iron out, new distractions to try out and other motivators to consider for your dog.

Continue the exercises

Continue regular practice sessions. Go over in your mind what you are going to do so that you can move from one exercise to another smoothly, without your dog sitting at the end of a lead waiting for you to reach a decision and getting bored in the process.

If during an exercise you suddenly realize you are doing it incorrectly, then finish off as best you can. It is extremely important that every practice session ends on a good note with you and the dog in a happy frame of mind. Remember always to help the dog get it right so you can praise him. Never be afraid to go back to the first steps of an exercise if your dog is experiencing difficulties or is distracted by new surroundings. Keep using your training aids: off-lead practice will come at a later stage.

Staying positive throughout

There are always variations but the fundamental principles of training have not really changed in practice. Some have acquired fancy-sounding names, but it would be true to say that training methods, as we have shown in this book, have become much more positive. The emphasis is now on teaching rather than punishing. If the method you are using works, do not try to change it. If you have followed our training methods and have at least given thought to where possible problems may occur, those problems can usually be forestalled. Certainly some dogs can be more difficult to train than others. The reasons are many, ranging from breed and age to temperament and background. Not every training method suits every dog, and not every dog suits every person.

Seeking more help

If you feel that the whole training course has been a constant battle and you have not achieved what you hoped for, you might seek further professional help from your dog training club or vet. Check out pages 186–187 which have details about where and how to seek further help. For instance, there are countless publications on the market covering every

aspect of dog ownership – from the dog's health to advanced competition sports. Some of these books are not available from high street stores, but can be obtained through specialist stockists – many of these have trade stands at championship breed shows. A visit to such a show will give you the opportunity to browse through the selection before making a purchase. The choice is staggering, but remember, however many books you read, unless you enjoy putting it all into practice, you and your dog won't achieve as much as you might like.

Dog training clubs

If you feel you need further help, try a dog training club. It is usually advisable to visit all the possible clubs, preferably in the first instance without your dog, so that you can look and listen to what is being said and done. Only if you are happy with the methods used and the experience available should you ask to join. Some clubs are aimed entirely at pet obedience and will be of no real benefit if you wish to compete; but they can be great fun and an opportunity for both you and your dog to socialize.

▲ Competitive Working Trials are based on police dog training and cover a number of exercises, including tracking. The dog tracks in a harness and on a long line rather than a lead. This dog's nose is well down as he follows the scent of the track layer.

want to know more?

Take it to the next level...

Go to...
- ▶ **Using rewards** – pages 152–159
- ▶ **Dog sports** – pages 160–177
- ▶ **Need to know more?** – pages 186–187

Other sources
- ▶ **Local dog training clubs**
  a good place to start looking for information and experience. Also try the the Telephone Directory, local vets, pet supply shops, local newspapers and word of mouth from fellow dog walkers.
- ▶ **Internet**
  visit www.the-kennel-club.org.uk

using

rewards

We stress throughout this book how important it is to praise your dog. Praise is always better than scolding. However, it is a fact of life that, for some dogs, food and toys are the only real motivation.

Treat exercises

Throughout the step-by-step lessons we have concentrated on using praise as the reward. However, food and toys are extremely useful tools which can be employed as bonus rewards or the prime motivator in some circumstances.

Handy access to treats

One difficulty of using food and toys is that you must have them handy to reward the dog. Many people find that co-ordinating the reward (food or toy) with the behaviour they are trying to encourage, takes much practice. The rewards can get buried in your pockets so that by the time they are found it is too late to reward the dog.

Tiny morsels

The treats should be just small enough to be a quick reward, not something he must chew for hours. The equivalent of children's dolly mixture sweets as opposed to gobstoppers! A variety is also useful to keep the dog interested, preferably things which the dog does not get all the time. If you have a really greedy dog you will probably be able to use the dog's normal dry food. It is surprising how much food can be used in a training session. Remember to watch your dog's weight. Regular weighing can be very useful to help you monitor his daily ration.

◄ Lured into the sit, this dog knows he will get no reward if he jumps up.

Tug-type toys

If you are using toys it is preferable to have something on a rope as a tug-type toy. These need to be a sensible size to fit in your pocket and can be given easily, and taken away after a quick game. Dogs love to play with a ball but the reward tends to be that the dog is playing on his own with his toy, not interacting with his owner. This can be a real problem in the early stages of training, particularly if he is not on the lead, as once the dog gets the toy he may decide he is not coming back. At least if the toy is on a rope, the handler can keep hold of it and play with the dog.

▲ The handler has used her leg as a bridge, and encouraged the dog to go down and crawl under of his own accord for the treat.

Luring into position

When starting with treats, they may need to be obvious to the dog as you are trying to lure him into position. Sometimes the dog may be so excited that he is leaping around without any thought as to what is required, such is his eagerness for the treat. Do keep calm and try to keep quiet, patiently waiting for him to stop. It should dawn on him eventually that his behaviour is not getting him the titbit. At this stage he will hopefully be open to suggestions. It is now that the handler should lure him into the desired position and the dog should then be rewarded instantly.

It can be helpful to manoeuvre the dog into position by altering your own body posture. Either lean to one side or the other, crouch down or even sit on the floor. A good example of this is teaching the dog to go into the 'down'. Some dogs initially object to the hands-on method, but will happily crawl under your arm or leg.

Reward exercises

Eventually the dog will realize that the bowl of treats or the special toy mean that he is going to play 'training games' and by now he will be responding reliably to familiar requests under these circumstances.

▼ Although we can see the toy it should be out of view for the dog, who is in front of the handler.

Around the house

Make sure requests include a verbal instruction, and not just a hand signal, with the food. Ideally use one-word commands when the dog is about to move into position. We do not want to teach him to expect lots of commands before he responds. You should be varying your location around the house and garden so that your dog realizes that the words mean the same thing regardless of place and that he will be rewarded. 'Sit' is still 'sit', whether it be by the front door or in the back garden.

Weaning off

It is now time to start weaning him off the lure. The treats should be prepared in advance or the toy put in a convenient position, which is not in plain view of the dog. When ready, the handler then asks the dog to do something which he is confident that the dog understands, using the same command and hand signal, but without the food. The dog might look slightly puzzled, as he does not see the reward in your hand, and a second command might be required. If the dog responds correctly, reward him immediately. If he doesn't, then you need to go back a few steps to help him succeed. Use the treat to lure him into the correct position, remembering to make sure to give the command at the same time.

Random reward

The basic principle of random rewarding is that the dog needs to be convinced that you always have a toy or treat somewhere, and that he never knows when it may appear. When we first reward the dog, be it with a favourite food or toy, we reward every successful action. In order to get a perpetually reliable response from him, we start dropping off the rewards. The first time this happens he will think it was a mistake on your part and he will try harder next time. So he gets his reward. Then we miss a couple, giving only verbal praise and patting. He may be slow on the third response but just when he thought it was a wasted effort, he gets his reward. By varying the intervals between verbal praise and the bonus rewards the dog will become more consistent in his response, hopeful that the next will be 'the one'.

Heelwork

This can be started off at home without a lead. The treat can be held in front of the dog's nose to encourage him to keep close to your left leg. Start with just a pace or two and reward, then three or four and so on. At this stage you are just getting your dog to follow. When the dog is on a collar and lead, as in our step by step (see pages 102–105), the lead can be in your left hand, leaving your right hand free to get treats from your pocket.

Recall to front

The front present exercise (see pages 120–125) is an ideal exercise in which to use food. The dog should not know that the handler has a tasty treat in his pocket. The dog should be at heel and as the handler steps back, calling the dog, the treat is produced. Even a hesitant dog will usually be pleased to come when called for a treat.

▲ Even very young puppies can be encouraged to follow at heel with a tasty morsel.

MUST KNOW

Testing you

Dogs are not machines and all of us have had dogs which have caused huge embarrassment at one time or another. Being able to laugh at yourself makes it easier to accept when your dog shows you up. Enjoy the moment before taking a step back in your training.

Earning it
NILIF: Nothing In Life Is Free – this attitude to living with a dog, or dogs, is becoming very popular. The dog must earn everything he wants, whether it be his food or your attention. He must at least sit when asked before getting anything from you.

Speeding it up

All exercises can get extremely boring and the dog's responses will slacken off, if simply repeated *ad nauseum*. It is much more fun for you and the dog if you can vary the basic routines, which will also help to improve the speed of your dog's response.

Many trainers consider that food is a calming reward and that toys are a reward to generate excitement. One way to encourage a fast, straight recall is to call your dog and instead of asking him to sit in front of you, send him through your legs. If you have his toy in your hands it can be thrown through your legs behind you, as you command 'go through' instead of sit. Then when you do a normal recall, hold your hands in the same position and the dog should recall speedily, in anticipation that on reaching you his toy will be thrown through your legs.

Reliable 'down', 'sit' and 'stand' positions are enormously useful and, in addition, are essential to many competition exercises.

Variation on 'fetch'

A great way to work on this, with an energetic dog who loves his toy, is while playing 'fetch'. The handler should pretend to throw the toy in one direction then the other, so that the dog

◄ Note the position of the hands as the toy has been thrown and the dog is commanded to 'go through'.

◄ An enthusiastic dog waits patiently for the handler to throw the ball.

starts to run backwards and forwards in front of them. A command (such as 'down', 'sit' or 'stand') should be given while the dog is close so that if the dog does not respond the handler can enforce it. Once the dog obeys, the handler instantly praises him, uses the release command and throws the toy. This can be repeated many times, while requesting alternative positions from the dog.

Harder variation

Another variation on this game is to keep the dog in a 'sit' or 'down' position while his toy is thrown. When the toy has landed and stopped rolling, the dog can be released to retrieve it. This is not as easy as it sounds, as most dogs are frantic to chase their toy. it may be necessary initially for you to use the lead to restrain the dog . Insist that he remain in position until being given a clear release command and allowing him to go.

want to know more?

Take it to the next level...

Go to...
- ▶ **Starting off** – pages 44–58
- ▶ **Dog sports** – pages 160–177
- ▶ **Need to know more?** – pages 186–187

Other sources
- ▶ **Local dog training clubs**
  a good place to start looking for information and experience. Also ask your fellow dog walkers.
- ▶ **Internet**
  visit www.doggiesolutions.co.uk or www.dogclub.co.uk or www.dogbasics.co.uk

dog

sports

If you've completed basic training successfully, you may feel your dog is ready for the world of dog sports. Events range from purely fun to seriously competitive, and combine key training methods with more athletic pursuits.

Competitive dog sports

The rules may vary from country to country around the world but the fun to be gained from competitive dog sports is universal. Obviously some breeds are more appropriate for certain sports – size for example, can be a restraint.

Taking training further

Before you get involved with any serious dog sport you must ensure that your dog is registered with the appropriate ruling canine society. Purebreds should have been registered as puppies on the main breed register; crossbreds and unregistered purebreds can usually be registered on a working register to allow them to take part in most competitions.

▼ One exercise in the Kennel Club Good Citizen Test is demonstrating good manners through doors and gates. This dog is sitting politely while the gate is opened.

You need to enter the majority of these competitions in advance, usually at least one month beforehand. There is also normally a minimum age at which a dog may compete. However, this is not to say that training cannot commence sooner! The progression through the levels may differ from sport to sport, some based on the age and experience of the dog, others requiring qualification from one level to the next. In many of the sports the dog can qualify and have initials after its registered name to signify the award gained. In some sports it is possible to gain the title 'Champion'.

Anyone wishing to find more detail on a particular sport should contact the Kennel Club or look on the internet (see pages 186–187).

Good Citizen Tests

Variations on these occur worldwide. They are not competitive tests as such, but there is a progression through the different levels. There are three levels in the UK: bronze, silver and gold.

◀ Handler and dog demonstrate the about turn in obedience heelwork. Note how the dog is close to the handler and paying close attention.

MUST KNOW

Obedience
Depending on the level of competition, heelwork may be done on or off the lead with changes of pace. The handler may, or may not, be allowed to give extra commands and praise while completing the exercise.

Basic social training

The tests are designed to encourage basic social training for all dogs, show or pet. The exercises are based on informal obedience behaviour, such as walking on a lead without pulling, coming when called and not barging through doors or gates. Your dog must also show that he is happy to be groomed or examined. Most of this should be taught as part of everyday life, making the bronze level readily attainable. A little more effort on behalf of the owner is required to obtain the silver and gold awards.

Obedience

One of the most popular sports is obedience as it doesn't require excessive equipment and it can be done with any breed. The rules and exercises differ around the world but usually include the following: heelwork, on and off the lead; recall; retrieving a dumb-bell or other article; staying in 'sit', 'stand' or 'down' positions; sending the dog away to a marked spot; scent discrimination and distance control. Heelwork may be at different paces and will include left, right and about turns. Judges look for precision in all exercises.

Basic control training

There are competitions for all sizes of dogs, with dogs and bitches competing on an equal level. These competitive events require the dog to be fit and agile. Basic control training is a must for all these off-lead sports.

Agility

Agility as a specific sport in its own right is often compared to show-jumping. A vast array of different obstacles has to be negotiated by the dog under guidance from his handler, including jumps, tunnels, see-saws and weave poles, to name just a few.

Out of the various canine sports, many people consider that agility is the most fun for both dogs and humans. It is possible to compete as an individual but is also popular as a team event. There are training clubs up and down the country.

▼ Great fun for playing with your dog on walks, and good exercise, dog discs come in a variety of colours and textures.

Dog disc sports

Another sport that requires a great athleticism in the dog is dog discs. These are very popular in the United States of America with different dog disc societies running competitions. The rules and classes tend to vary among the societies. The type and make of dog disc may be specified, while the competition can be either a distance contest or an accuracy contest. In addition, there is a freestyle variation of the sport which is a little like heelwork to music!

Obviously for this type of exercise the dog must be physically fit. There is usually a minimum age at which a dog can compete and a good recall and retrieve are essential. This is a great spectator sport and whole families often attend events to offer support.

Flyball

Another fun activity you can enjoy with your dog closely is flyball. It follows agility in popularity and involves teams running against each other and the clock, and is noisy and lively. It is a relay race in which each dog has to race over a line of small hurdles, to the fly-ball box.

The dog presses a pedal on the box which releases a tennis ball into the air. The dog must catch the ball and race back over the hurdles, to its handler waiting at the start/finish line and then the next dog is released. Numbers can vary in the team – it is usually left to the discretion of the event organiser. Quite often agility clubs run fly-ball as well.

Fit to train

For all these competitive sports it is a good thing if the handler is fit and active! You will probably find, though, that the preparation you put in for these sports will keep you both in good shape.

▲ Agility obstacles include a dog walk. The dog must touch the yellow steps at the start and finish.

MUST KNOW

Safety
Most dogs adore chasing a ball, but choose carefully. It must be the right size for your dog to catch in his jaws but not so small that he might swallow it.

▶ Working trials

Working trials are frequently confused with field trials and sheepdog trials, both of which are totally different. Working trials are a sport specific to the UK, although Europe and North America have similar exercises with corresponding titles that may be used after the dog's registered name.

The stakes

The working trials exercises are designed to test a dog's working ability and the competitions are very popular with dog handlers from the police and armed forces, as well as pet owners. There are five stakes: in the lower two stakes the agility equipment is graded to the height of the dog. In the higher stakes, a dog must be able to scale 1.83m (6ft), clear a 2.75m (9ft) long jump and clear a 0.92m (3ft) high hurdle.

This means that while the lower stakes are open to most breeds. In reality the jumps restrict the competition in the higher levels to medium and large dogs. In the UK the exercises are grouped together and an overall percentage of marks must be gained in each group to get a qualifying certificate.

Grouped exercises

In North America the exercises are treated as individual competitions so that a dog may achieve a tracking dog certificate which does not include the agility and other control exercises used in the UK. The exercises are grouped into obedience, agility and nose work sections.

▶ This dog is on the 1.83 metre (6ft) scale. He will wait on the other side in the nominated position until recalled back over the scale by his handler. Part of the long jump is visible in the background.

In C.D. (Companion Dog) the lowest stake, the nose work consists of a property search square. All the other stakes also have a track, which will not be less than 0.8km (half a mile) long and will include turns and articles that need to be found. The track pattern will be unknown by the handler and will have been 'put down' by a track layer earlier. The age of the track ranges from 30 minutes old to three hours old depending on the stake being worked.

Generally speaking the higher the level of competition the more legs (changes of direction) are involved, and the smaller the articles.

Bloodhounds

Bloodhounds have their own trials, which are based primarily on tracking. They have their own rules and regulations. The dogs are frequently without a line, and their tracking is across varied terrain, and can cross a number of fields before the end is reached. The runner who has laid the track has then to be identified by the dog at the end of the track.

◀ The dog tracks in a harness with a long line rather than a lead. This dog's nose is well down as he follows the scent of the track layer.

Breed shows

As the name implies, these are beauty contests for dogs. Assuming that the registered dog is of show quality then this sport is open to all.

The breed standard

All around the world the principle behind breed show is the same: judges are looking for the dog that, in their view, comes closest to the breed standard, which is the written blueprint for the breed.

Classifications vary between countries but generally have age-related classes, for example puppy or junior; and award-related classes based on the prizes a dog has already gained. The 'Best of Breed' is selected from the winners of the breed classes, the systems varying slightly worldwide. The best of each breed then competes for 'Best In Group' and the best of each group competes for 'Best In Show'.

▼ Handlers standing their dogs for the judge to view at an outdoor breed show.

▶ A typical carpeted ring at a large indoor breed show. This is a special class with a variety of breeds competing.

Many varied classifications

Under some systems there may be special classes in which different breeds compete against each other. These may be for dogs with working qualifications or they may be sponsored by major dog food manufacturers.

The rules and regulations vary from country to country. The FCI, for example, has a ten group system where the UK only has seven groups. See the glossary (pages 182–185) for more details of breeds and groups.

Training for breed showing

Even before the dog gets to a show, there is an enormous amount of work to do. The dog must be in tip-top condition, gleaming with health and vitality. Active breeds will need plenty of regular exercise to keep them well-muscled. Each dog's coat is groomed according to its type, and its teeth and nails will also have received attention.

Training for breed showing requires a reasonable amount of work to get the dog to show-off to best advantage. The work is built on basic exercises. The dog must stand, preferably still, so that the judge can admire his good qualities. The dog must also be amenable to handling so that the judge can examine him more closely. The dog must move freely in a controlled manner so that his movement can be observed from various angles.

Ring-craft classes

Breed-show training can be taught at ring-craft classes, where you can experience a pretend show class. Ring-craft classes are a good place for dogs and handlers to learn about the etiquette of the show ring. They are also a good place for young dogs to become accustomed to the routine. At shows dogs can be handled by their owners, which tends to be the norm in the UK for most breeds. Dogs can also be handled in the ring by a professional handler if preferred, which is quite common in North America.

▶ Further trials

Whether you use classical, country and western, or pop, heelwork to music makes off-lead training a really fun work out. Gundog trials, by contrast, are more seriously inclined.

Heelwork to music

The principle element of heelwork to music is the dog working off lead at heel on the right or left hand side of the handler, or in other movements maintaining close position. Heelwork is the substantial part of the routine. This discipline tests the dog's ability to keep its shoulder reasonably close to

◀ Heelwork to music has moved on from being a sport that is just about heelwork. Some routines may be purely freestyle, (not relying on the dog to walk in the heelwork position).

the left or right knee of the handler, who moves smartly at any suitable pace. Additional movements should be included in the routine and be linked by heelwork. A freestyle routine will contain movements in any position including heelwork, but only as a minimal part of the routine. Freestyle routines allow those who do not work in obedience to compete on an equal footing with those that do, as it also allows for a different interpretation of the obedience communication between handler and dog.

Gundogs

Field trials and gundog working tests have developed to test the working ability of gundogs in competitive conditions. These conditions – and the game pursued – vary from rabbit and hares to partridges and pheasants in the UK, to elk in Finland and raccoons in North America.

Gundog working tests involve usually using either a dummy (a sand-filled canvas bag) or cold game. To compete, the gundog owners often need to be members of the organizing society. The tests are based on the inherent traits of the breed of dog.

▼ Many owners of gundog breeds enjoy competing in working tests as a hobby. Breed show enthusiasts like to know that their gundog breeds have retained working ability, be it tracking, retrieving, pointing or flushing game and use the working tests to confirm this.

Companion Dog Shows

Companion Dog Shows are the first taste of competitive obedience for many people. The fact that the entries are handed in on the day gives the newcomer a chance to see what is expected and then decide whether to have a go.

Origins

In the past, Companion Dog Shows used to be called Exemption Dog Shows as they were considered to be exempt from the usual Kennel Club Rules governing competitions, even though they still had to have a licence from the Kennel Club. Societies registered with the Kennel Club were not eligible to run these fun shows. They were mainly organized by small clubs and the funds raised were not intended for use by the society. Now called Companion Dog Shows, they are still run primarily to raise funds for good causes. Registered societies are now able to hold Companion Dog Shows if they wish. They can also keep 50 per cent of any profit for the registered society holding the event.

Open to all dogs

Companion Dog Shows are open to all breeds of dog; they do not need to be registered or even of a recognized breed to compete. The dogs must be a minimum of six months old to enter. Entries are taken on the day, as compared to Breed Shows where the entries close weeks in advance. Most events hold show classes for which the Kennel Club gives clear guidelines for the titles. They are mixed classes, generally any variety in a particular breed group, for example Any Variety Gundog. The other split is into age groups - puppy, junior, open or veteran. In any event there will be a variety of breeds in the ring. These dogs will all appear to be recognized pedigree breeds but they need not be dogs registered with the Kennel Club. This is an excellent way to introduce young show prospects to the competition ring. Successful top-winning show dogs are normally barred from competing at Companion Dog Shows.

Triers, starters and flyers

Sometimes there are obedience classes at these events. These are at the organizers' discretion and have titles such as triers, starters and flyers. The exercises will be similar to the serious obedience competitions but not necessarily so stringent. The Kennel Club guidelines specifically state that

the titles and tests should differ from those laid down in the Kennel Club Rules and Regulations. The standard of work from the dogs can be hugely variable from absolute beginner (both dogs and handlers) to much more stylish. Many first timers get the bug at such shows and discover the world of open competitions – and a full-time hobby.

▲ A judge watches the movement of a Cocker Spaniel in this Any Variety Gundog class.

Fun classes

Companion Dog Shows would not be complete without the fun classes. These are left to the organizers' imaginations and can be Dog with the Waggiest Tail, Best Rescue or Dog in Best Condition to name but a few. Best Fancy Dress and Dog Most Like its Owner generally produce some humorous entries.

Children can take part and may enjoy handling the family pet, particularly if the judge is a well-known personality, which is often the case in these fun classes. As it is such a relaxed event the majority of people will be happy to chat and give personal experience of dog-ownership.

MUST KNOW

Social skills
A companion show is a good place to practise basic puppy training, even if you don't enter the ring! Most people your puppy meets will be dog-minded with, hopefully, well-mannered dogs.

DOG SPORTS

173

▶ Racing

Racing has its origins in hunting and coursing way back before the Christian Era. Greyhounds chasing mechanical rabbits as a competitive sport originated in the United States.

▲ Whippets are smaller than greyhounds and can have small starting boxes but sometimes they are just held by their owners or a helper, and then released to chase the fur-covered mechanical rabbit.

Classic racing

Greyhound-type dogs have been with man for centuries, and certainly existed in the time of the Ancient Egyptian pharaohs. They varied in size and weight depending on what game they were being used to catch. All were bred for speed. Early races would simply have involved seeing which dog was first to catch the prey (which was then destined for the pot). The races subsequently developed into competitions.

Classic greyhound racing is a specialist sport, although amateurs can get involved and can be very successful. Training is very intensive and not normally undertaken at home. Even though privately owned, most greyhounds are kept in racing kennels where they will be trained to get them physically fit to race. Other breeds also race although not in such a commercial fashion.

Other breeds

Afghans, whippets, lurchers and terriers all have racing events held for them. These are normally organized by field sport societies or the specific breed clubs. Whatever the breed, the winner is the first across the finish line – assuming there have been no fouls *en route*!

Afghans frequently use greyhound tracks, including the starting boxes and the proper rabbit. Whippets and lurchers are ragged – encouraged to the end of the race by their owner or handler waving a rag or towel beyond the finishing line.

MUST KNOW

Earthdogs
Dogs bred to hunt vermin underground have their own competitions. Tunnels are constructed so dogs can replicate the task of ratting. These are minority sports mostly known within the circles of the breed clubs.

Terriers

Terrier racing is noisy and fast, mimicking the ratting background of most terriers. Tracks are frequently made using straw bales as barriers. These races occur at game fairs and countryside events. With the owners shouting encouragement to their dogs, and the noise generated by the terriers themselves amid the general air of chaos, it can be quite difficult to actually tell which dog won the race!

Sledding and skijoring

Most traditional dog sledding involves a dog or dogs pulling a sled. This can be a fun pastime even without racing. Depending on country and conditions the length of races will vary from quite short distances with several races being held on one day, to the famous Iditarod race across hundreds of miles of Alaskan wilderness. Even in countries with a lack of snow, fun can be had with wheeled rigs. Traditionally husky-type breeds are associated with sledding. However in reality all sorts of breeds are used.

The United States of America and Canada have a variation of sledding called skijoring in which a person on skis is pulled on a harness and line connected to the dog. Skijoring is a fun way to enjoy exercise with one or two dogs. During the summer, you can use your skijoring system to roller skate with your dog. (Please use appropriate padding and a helmet!) To make the activity safe and fun, you should always use a padded belt, a shock absorbing line and a quick release clip.

▲ When the skijoring handler receives the judge's signal to start, the helpers will release this pair of eager huskies.

▲ A Newfoundland performing a rescue. Sometimes a large doll is used to represent the child.

▼ This German Shepherd Dog is barking to hold the helper in his hide until rejoined by his handler, as part of a protection sport exercise.

Other events

All sorts of other events exist for dogs and their owners. Some are highly specialized and require much expert tuition before participation. Others are more relaxed and can be indulged in as a gentle hobby.

Newfoundland events

Bred as water-rescue dogs, Newfoundlands retrieved boat ropes or people who had fallen in the water. Newfoundland clubs run events to demonstrate that the dogs still have the inherited capability to perform water rescues. Newfoundlands are also able to tow a small rowing boat to shore, should the oars be lost or the rower incapacitated.

Schutzhund tests

Schutzhund began as a test for working dogs, its purpose being to determine which dogs should be used for breeding. The dog's mental stability, endurance, physical structure, ability to follow a scent, willingness to work, courage and trainability are all assessed in the tests. It has now become a very popular sport.

Handlers and dogs are judged in three areas: tracking, obedience and protection. Dogs must pass a temperament test and obtain a BH (Begleithundprufung) degree to be able to compete. A BH is a test of character and obedience. All three phases are clearly defined: heelwork patterns and track patterns and the protection work routine are always the same. The handler knows exactly what he needs to train for in each section.

Protection disciplines

Mondio, KNPV and French Ringsport are three primarily protection disciplines popular in Europe and America. Variations exist across the globe.

It is of paramount importance that dogs trained in protection sports have a sound temperament and a thorough grounding in obedience.

Herding

The classic image of herding is the Border Collie and a flock of sheep. This has turned into a popular test for many dogs, primarily in the pastoral breed group. Mainly sheep or cattle are used, although ducks may be used as a starter to test basic herding instincts. This is quite hard to get into as farmers do not wish their valuable stock to be bitten or frightened by amateur handlers and inexperienced dogs. Many of the participants in competitions will have working experience of livestock and have connections in the farming community. The sport gained a popular following with the hugely successful British television series 'One Man and His Dog'.

In some countries the breed clubs run tests so that owners or breeders can confirm that their dogs still have the inherent capability to do the job they were originally bred for.

▲ An Australian Cattle Dog heeling low to move the stock. In Britain, Sheepdog Trials with Border Collies or Working Sheepdogs, were so popular the heats were televised, and became compelling weekly viewing.

want to know **more?**

Take it to the next level...

Go to...
▶ **Using rewards** – pages 152–159
▶ **Dog essentials** – pages 178–181
▶ **Need to know more?** – pages 186–187

Other sources
▶ **Magazines**
  Working Trials Monthly, Dog Monthly, Your Dog, Our Dogs, Dog World and other publications are a great resource for information on dog sports
▶ **Internet**
  a minefield but bona fide dog-related sports sites are www.workingtrials.co.uk; www.agilitynet.com; www.flyball.org.uk

dog

essentials

Hopefully you are now enjoying the mutual benefits of a well-trained dog. To help you on the road to a wider world of training experiences the following pages give you some essential pointers.

▶ Travelling in safety

Well-behaved dogs are usually accepted as passengers on buses and trains but the majority of us travel mainly by car with our pets. This poses many potential hazards.

Restraining the dog

Far too many dogs are left loose in the car while it is in motion. Most countries' law will state something to the effect that the dog should be restrained safely to prevent him interfering with the driver. This takes no real account of the safety of the dog in the event of an accident, not to mention the risk of escape via insecure doors or window opened for ventilation.

The most obvious form of restraint is to tie the dog up using the lead, making sure that the collar is loose so that the dog will not choke. Personally we feel other methods are better as it is not unknown for the dog to manage to hang itself on the head-rests or door handles when secured in this way. While he is accompanied in the car, a harness which fixes to the seat belt may be a useful tool as it will prevent the dog being flung around in the event of an accident. The dog must be taught how to behave while wearing the harness otherwise he may become a distraction to the driver.

The old-fashioned dog guard which fits behind the seat is still popular and prevents the dog accessing the driver. It must be securely fitted, bolted in is best. However it still allows the dog to be thrown around and does not prevent him jumping out of the boot when it is opened.

Travel crates

There are two types of travel crate, collapsible or rigid. Sturdy collapsible crates can be secured in position so that they do not move around in the

▼ This medium-size dog is ready to go, wearing a car harness which is attached to the seat belt.

car. They will restrain the dog, giving him a smaller area while travelling and will offer some protection in the event of a crash. They can also be removed easily from the car for storage or alternative use. Rigid cages are usually custom-made for the model of car. They are very heavy, and can only be removed with difficulty, but offer the best protection and security for the dog. Most have emergency access doors on either side.

Most dogs will travel happily in these, viewing them as cosy dens of their own, especially if they were crate-trained in the house as puppies.

▲ Dogs loose in the back of the utility vehicle – a popular mode of travel in Australia on farms and off-road, but not recommended on public roads!

◀ Travel crates are probably the ideal way for dogs to travel: safe for them and for the driver.

CHECKLIST

Dos and Don'ts

- Do make sure the puppy has been given the opportunity to relieve himself before travelling in the car.
- Don't feed just before a car journey, especially a long one. Some dogs are carsick – be patient, most grow out of it given time and understanding.
- Do make sure that your dog will not jump out of the car until you command him. Even in a car park it can be dangerous if the dog leaps out suddenly.
- Always ensure that your dog is not left in the car without ventilation, even in winter. The temperature can build up quickly on a sunny day.
- First journeys for puppies should be short with something enjoyable at the end – like a walk.

Glossary of terms

Agility
Dog sport often compared to showjumping.

AKC
American Kennel Club.

Angulation
Refers to angles created by bones meeting at various joints, especially the shoulder, stifles and hock. 'Well angulated' or 'well turned' describes dogs exhibiting the correct range of angulations for their breed.

Anticipation
What dogs do and shouldn't in obedience training, e.g. acting in anticipation of the command before receiving it.

Balanced
Refers to a pleasingly symmetrical dog in terms of its various features.

Bandy legs
Legs that are bent outwards.

Beard
Wiry whiskers as seen in most wire-haired breeds but also other breeds.

Best in Show
Animal judged to be the best of all the breeds in a given show. Also title of humorous tongue-in-cheek dog-show movie (2000) from the makers of *This Is Spinal Tap*.

Bitch
Female dog.

Bite
Relative position of the upper and lower teeth when the dog's mouth is closed.

Blaze
White stripe running up the dog's face or forehead.

Bobtail
Naturally short-tailed or docked dog. Also another name for the Old English Sheepdog.

Bone
Used to describe the size of the bone in a dog (a greyhound would be light-boned, a wolfhound heavy-boned).

Breed
Type of dog; usually refers to a variety of purebred dog – a dog or bitch with a pedigree.

Brindle
Coat colour made of stripes of light and dark hairs.

Brisket
Front of the chest between the forelegs.

Button ear
Ear that drops over in front, with tip drooping over.

Canine
Term referring to all things to do with dogs, wolves, foxes, jackals and other members of that family (as in canis familiaris).

Canine teeth
Otherwise known as the fangs: the long, pointy ones.

Challenge certificates
Awarded to the top dog and bitch in some UK shows. In other countries points are awarded.

Champion
Exact definition varies from kennel club to kennel club, but generally refers to a dog who has won the required amount of Challenge certificates or points in the relative disciplines.

Check chain/collar
Chain or leather collar fitted to the dog's neck that can be tightened or loosened by hand pressure applied by the handler. A useful training aid.

Choke chain
This is a check chain upside down and is cruel!

Clicker
Small training device that makes a clicking noise when you apply pressure with your thumb.

Collar
Band worn around a dog's neck to which a lead can be attached to control a dog.

Companion dog
One that keeps you company, also the name of a breed group.

Crossbred
Puppy of purebred parents of different breeds.

Dew claw
Claw on the inside of the dog's leg, usually removed but kept for some breeds.

Dewlap
Loose hanging skin under the dog's throat most obviously in a bloodhound.

Disc, throwing
Familiar-looking beach toy adapted for canine agility tests.

Docking

Shortening the tail by surgical cut. Some breed standards demand this but it is in the process of being outlawed.

Dog

Male of the species, as opposed to the bitch (female).

Dog show

Exhibition at which dogs are judged according to recognized standards for that particular kennel club. Also usually attracts exhibitors of dog supplies, petcare, foodstuffs, accessories, insurance, and so on.

Down

When the dog lies flat.

Down stay

Dog remaining in the 'down' position until told to move.

Elbow out

Where the joint at the top of the forearm points away from the body – a fault found in many breeds.

Faking

When undesirable features of a dog are hidden from the judges of a dog show.

Fast down

Dog going 'down' very quickly from the 'stand'.

FCI

Fédération Cynologique Internationale – one of the ruling bodies in the canine world.

Fetch

Command to retrieve an object and the act of doing it (as a game or training technique).

Field trial

Competition for gundogs.

Flyball

Relay competition retrieving balls over hurdles.

Front present

Exercise where the dog is called to come in to the front of the handler.

Gait

Style of movement e.g. running or trotting.

Gallop

Fastest dog gait.

Game

Birds or other animal traditionally hunted by dogs.

Gazehound

Hound that hunts using sight (rather than smell); also called sighthound.

GDBA

Guide Dogs for the Blind Association, breeder and trainer of dogs to assist the blind.

Grizzle

Bluish-grey coat colour.

Groom

To comb, brush, trim and generally prepare a dog's coat (for pleasure or show).

Guard hairs

Longer, stiffer hairs that protect the soft undercoat.

Gun dogs

Dogs, such as setters, pointers and retrievers, trained to assist hunter in the field.

Hackles

Hair on the neck and back raised by instinct when dog is agitated, especially frightened or aggressive.

Handler

Someone who handles the dog for you – the person at the other end of the lead.

Harness

Straps shaped around the shoulders and chest to which other equipment can be attached. Also the term for a car restraint for dogs.

HD or Hip dysplasia

Inherited condition of the bone in the hip joint, where the thigh bone does not fit properly into the pelvis.

Heat

When the female is in season. Technically called oestrus. This normally occurs every six months.

Heelwork

The act of the dog following close to your heel.

Heelwork to music

Competition involving the dog remaining primarily close to your left leg while moving in time to music.

Height

For a dog this is measured from the withers to the ground in normal stance.

Judge

Person adjudicating dog show competition.

Kennel Club, The (KC)

Ruling canine body in the UK.

Kennel

Structure where dog is kept and made to feel safe. Can be indoors or outdoors. Also boarding place for dogs.

KNVP
Royal Dutch Policedog Association, which provides trained dogs for police, military and rescue organizations.

Lead
Safety line used to control a dog.

Long line
Excessively long lead used for some training problems.

Merle
Usually refers to patches of light and dark colours on a dog's coat.

Milk teeth
Dog's baby teeth. Puppies lose these from the age of four to six months. A dog should have 42 adult teeth.

Mongrel
Dog who comes from parents of mixed breeding.

Muzzle
Device to prevent biting, put over the dog's face; also the part of the dog's head that includes the mouth and nose.

Obedient
What a dog should be, especially after training.

Obstacles
Commonly used in Agility to refer to all the different pieces of equipment which the dog has to negotiate.

Off lead
Hopefully in control, without a lead attached to the dog.

On lead
When the dog is attached to his lead.

Pacing
Two-time gait in which the two feet on one side advance together, followed by the two feet on the other side.

Pedigree
Written certificate authenticating a dog's lineage as being purebred over generations.

Play retrieve
Fun game in which the dog returns to owner with various objects that the owner has thrown for him.

Police dog
Dog used in the police forces to aid in the detection of crime and enforcing the law.

Professional handler
Person who shows dogs in the ring for the owner for a fee.

Pulse rate
Speed at which the heart beats: for dogs this is 70–100 beats per minute. Larger breeds generally have a slower rate.

Purebred
Dog with both parents from the same breed. A dog can be purebred without a pedigree.

Racing
Competition to find the fastest dog or team.

Register
To record the details of a dog's breeding with the respective kennel club.

Retrieve
To bring back some shot game, but nowadays used to denote fetching any object chosen by the handler.

Sable
Coat colour produced by the black-tipped hairs on a background of another colour.

Saddle
Solid area of colour over the shoulder and back of a dog, like a horse's saddle.

Scale
High wall (2m/6ft) which the dog has to get over in some competitions such as Working Trials.

Scent
Odour left by a dog to mark out its territory, or the trail that it follows when tracking.

Schutzhund
Sport consisting of Protection, Obedience and Tracking; also used as an assessment for suitability for breeding (particularly for German Shepherd Dogs).

Single tracking
When the dog's pads converge to a central line in fast motion. It is more natural in longer-legged dogs than with shorter, squatter dogs. The legs angle in towards a central line beneath the body – the greater the speed, the closer they come together.

Sit
When the dog has its bottom on the ground.

Sit stay
Dog remaining with bottom on ground until released

Slicker brush
Piece of equipment with short teeth, usually wire, for grooming dogs.

Smooth coat
Short, sleek hair lying close to the skin.

Stack
Position in which handlers normally place their dogs in the show ring. Also called stance.

Stand
For a dog to remain stationary with all four feet on the ground.

Stilted
A stiff, awkward gait.

Temperature
Dog's normal body temperature: this is 100.9–101.7° Fahrenheit (38.3–38.7° Centigrade).

Type
Characteristics that make up and help to define a breed. The qualities conforming to a Breed standard.

Undercoat
Soft, dense hair under the longer outer hair.

Varminty
Bright alert expression, often seen in terriers.

Wait
Means 'remain in that position but pay attention' in training.

Watch
When the dog makes eye contact with the handler or owner.

Wire haired
Tough, dense coat often associated with terriers.

Withers
Highest point of the dog's shoulder, and from where the dog's height is measured.

Working trials
Tests based on police dog training in the UK involving tracking, obedience, agility and searching.

Parts of a dog

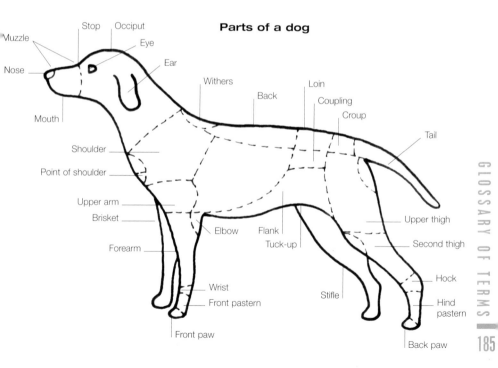

Muzzle, Stop, Occiput, Eye, Ear, Nose, Mouth, Withers, Back, Loin, Coupling, Croup, Tail, Shoulder, Point of shoulder, Upper arm, Brisket, Elbow, Flank, Tuck-up, Upper thigh, Second thigh, Forearm, Wrist, Front pastern, Stifle, Hock, Hind pastern, Front paw, Back paw

Need to know more?

The following organizations will be of use for those seeking further advice and information on dogs and dog training.

Clubs and Associations

Association of Pet Behaviour Counsellors
P.O Box 46l
Worcester, WR8 9YS

tel 01386 751151
fax 01386 750743
www.apbc.org.uk

An international network of experienced and qualified pet behaviour counsellors.

Battersea Dogs Home
4 Battersea Park Road, Battersea,
London, SW8 4AA

tel 0207 6223626
fax 0207 6226451
www.dogshome.org

UK's largest, probably best-known, rescue centre for dogs and cats.

British Veterinary Association
7 Mansfield Street, London W1

tel 0207 6366541
fax 0207 4362970
www.bva.co.uk

National representative body for the British veterinary profession.

The Guide Dog for the Blind Association
Burghfield Common, Reading,
Berkshire, RG7 3YG

tel 0118 9835555
www.guidedogs.org.uk

'Leading' charity whose publications are of use to anyone training a dog.

The Kennel Club
1–5 Clarges Street, Piccadilly,
London, W1J 8AB

tel 0870 606 6750
fax 0207 518 1058
www.the-kennel-club.org.uk
UK ruling body on canine matters.

Pet Food Manufacturer's Association (UK)
20 Bedford Street, Covent Garden,
London, WC2E 9HP

tel 0207 3799009
fax 0207 3798008

Aims to be the credible voice of a responsible pet food industry.

Pet Passport – contact DEFRA Information Resource Centre,
Lower Ground Floor, Ergon House,
c/o Nobel House, 17 Smith Square,
London SW1P 3JR

tel 0207 2386951
fax 0207 2386609
www.defra.gov.uk

Anyone wishing to travel with their dog, into or out of the UK, should contact DEFRA for information.

Pets As Therapy (PAT)
3 Grange Farm Cottages, Wycombe
Road, Saunderton, Princes
Risborough, Bucks, HP27 9NS

tel 0870 240 1239
fax 0870 706 2562
www.petsastherapy.org

People of all ages and disabilities can enjoy the services of PAT Dog visits.

Magazines and newspapers

Your Dog BPG (Stamford) Ltd.
33 Broad Street, Stamford,
Lincolnshire PE9 1RB

tel 01780 766199
fax 01780 754744
www.yourdog.co.uk

One of Britain's best-selling monthly dog magazines.

Our Dogs
5 Oxford Road Station Approach,
Manchester M60 1SX

www.ourdogs.co.uk

Weekly newspaper primarily for breed shows.

Dog World
Somerfield House, Wotton Road,
Ashford, Kent, TN23 6LW

www.dogworld.co.uk

Another weekly newspaper dedicated to dogs.

Dogs Monthly
Ascot House, High Street, Ascot,
Berkshire SL5 7JG

tel: 0870 7308433
fax: 0870 7308431

Collection of articles for all dog lovers.

Working Trials Monthly
26 Broad Lane, Betteshanger, Kent,
CT14 0LX

tel/fax: 01304 614708.

A must for Working Trials competitors.

Useful dog-related web sites

www.fediaf.org
European Pet Food Industry Federation

www.doglaw.co.uk
Experienced specialist law firm in all canine matters.

www.apdt.co.uk
Association of Pet Dog Trainers, useful articles on training classes and problems.

www.cpiuk.org
Canine partners for independence.

www.dogsforthedisabled.org
Canine partners for the disabled.

www.hearing-dogs.co.uk
Hearing dogs for deaf people.

www.agilitynet.com
Information for agility enthusiasts.

www.workingtrials.co.uk
Information for working trial enthusiasts.

www.schutzhund.fsnet.co.uk
British Schutzhund Association.

www.obedienceuk.com
A must for all obedience enthusiasts.

www.flyball.org.uk
Rules and regulations and everything else you need to know about flyball.

www.caninefreestylegb.com
A site for those who love dogs and music.

www.clickandtreat.com
Gary Wilkes expertise on clicker training on-line.

www.dog-n-field.co.uk
Everything gundog.

www.flyingdogpress.com
Excellent site for training articles and information.

Helpful dog books

The Family Dog
by John Holmes (Popular Dogs Publishing Co. 1975)

This, along with other books by John Holmes, has good basic information on living with a dog.

Dogs Behaving Badly: A Practical Problem Solver
by Gwen Bailey (Collins 2004)

Useful handbook for any dog owner experiencing behavioural or training problems by dog behaviourist,

How to Own a Sensible Dog
by Joyce Stranger (Corgi Books 1981)

An interesting book drawing on the author's experience of living with different dogs and their problems.

Don't Shoot the Dog
by Karen Pryor (Bantam Books 1985)

Excellent introduction to the principles of clicker training from Karen Pryor, who introduced the technique to dog trainers.

Tracking Dog
by Glen Johnson (Arner Publications 1975)

Good book for tracking enthusiasts everywhere. The week-by-week progress charts are very good.

How to be Your Dog's Best Friend
by The Monks of New Skete (Little, Brown & Co. Publishing 1978)

Insight on the monks and their methods of rearing and training dogs, primarily German Shepherds.

The Encyclopaedia of the Dog
by Bruce Fogle (Dorling Kindersley 1995)

A comprehensive guide to the dog breeds of the world, super photos.

Veterinary Notes for Dog Owners
by Trevor Turner (Popular Dogs Publishing Co. 1990)

Covers most common ailments without being too technical.

Jumping from A to Z
by M. Christine Zink (Canine Sports Productions 1995)

A must for all sport dog owners who need to keep their dogs fit, as well as for Agility enthusiasts.

An Eye for a Dog
by Robert Cole (Dogwise 2004)

Even if you are not going to show or breed, this well-laid out, easy to follow book is worth reading.

Puppy Training The Guide Dogs Way
by Julia Barnes (Ringpress 2004)

An excellent book with the emphasis on puppy rearing to produce a happy family dog. Particularly interesting are the puppy assessments.

Collins Dog Showing
by Robert Killick (Collins 2003)

Helpful on all aspects of dog showing with insider tips to winning and advice on the breeds, the rules and the shows.

Dima's Dog School
by Dima Yeremenko and Emily Randolph (Piatkus Books 2004)

Primarily using food as a reward, Dima has an easy style that is fun as well as educational.

How to Talk with Your Dog
by David Alderton (Collins 2004)

A guide to understanding and communicating with your dog.

The Working Trial Dog
by Peter Lewis (Popular Dogs)

Anyone using scent exercises as a game will find this book interesting, even though it is intended for Working Trials competitors.

Collins Gem – Dog Training
by Gwen Bailey (Collins 2004)

Information-packed pocket guide.

Collins Gem – Dogs
by Wendy Boorer (Collins 1999)

Well-illustrated dog mini-book.

▶ Index

Acknowledgements

Indexer: Patricia Hymans

Picture credits All pictures by Tracy Morgan Animal Photography except p19, 21, 142, 168, 173 from Collins Dog Showing by Robert Killick (2003); p13, 22, 23, 35, 38, 42, 43, 60, 71, 163, 166, 175, 176, 177 Stella Smyth; p171 Susan Redshaw, p47, 169 James Harrison; p181 Lady Huntingdon. Every effort has been made to credit the original source photographers.

Thank you to the following models: Jennie Bergh-Roose, Dennis Roose, Alex Barry, Tom Kinsey, Jennifer Reagan, Penny Harrison; also to Stephanie and Adam Carpenter. Frank Gray and Travis (Australian Shepherd Dog), Mindy Gittoes and Conker (Welsh Terrier.), Kathy, Emma and Sophie Chapman and Rosie (Labrador), Lisa White and Woody (Golden Retirever), Caroline Graham and Piglet (Cross-breed), Sue Cragie and Kip and Zena (Rhodesian Ridgeback). Lady Huntingdon and her puppy (Australian Cattle Dog). Other dog models:Tikka (Tracy's Cocker Spaniel)

The authors' dogs:
German Shepherd Dogs: Chaos (Olderhill Abeth at Sarsway Companion Dog Excellent, Utility Dog Excellent, Working Dog Excellent, Tracking Dog Excellent) 1999–2003.
Hudson (Sarsway Arak Companion Dog Excellent, Utility Dog Excellent, Working Dog Excellent, Tracking Dog Excellent)
Mallik (Sarsway Ardent Companion Dog Excellent, Utility Dog Excellent, Working Dog Excellent, Tracking Dog)
Logan (Conquell Qwango Companion Dog Excellent, Utility Dog Excellent)
Ji (Toilers Timo at Sarsway Companion Dog Excellent, Utility Dog Excellent, Working Dog Excellent, Tracking Dog)
Raki (Conquell Rakilah)
Australian Cattle Dogs: Smoky (Morrow Blue Aborigine Companion Dog Excellent, Utility Dog Excellent, Working Dog Excellent, Tracking Dog Excellent) 1991-2003
Kynie (Warrigal Blue Kookynie at Morrow Companion Dog, Utility Dog Excellent, Working Dog Excellent, Tracking Dog)
Mulga (Morrow Red Chakola Companion Dog Excellent, Utility Dog Excellent, Working Dog, Tracking Dog)
Skippy (Morrow Red Coolibah)
Yarae (Morrow Diamond Dreaming)
Toodyay (Morrow Blue Flinders)
Also to Moss End Garden Centre Ltd for the loan of training equipment. Straid Veterinary Hospital for the use of the Vet's Coat

Websites
Every effort has been made to source suitable websites related to dogs and dog training. The authors, packagers and publishers cannot be held responsible for exposure to internet sites that may have become inappropriate or contain offensive or harmful material or content. Nor can they be held liable for any damage or loss caused by viruses as a result of browsing the recommended websites.

Collins need to know?

Further titles in Collins' practical and accessible **Need to Know?** series:

Digital photography
All the kit, techniques and tips you need to take great photographs

192pp   £8.99
PB   0 00 718031 4

Golf
All the kit, techniques and inspiration to get into the game

192pp   £8.99
PB   0 00 718037 3

Zodiac types
Yourself, your friends and your family revealed

192pp   £7.99
PB   0 00 718038 1

Watercolour
All the kit, techniques and inspiration you need to get into painting

192pp   £8.99
PB   0 00 718032 2

Card games
All the rules and tips you need to start playing over 60 card games

192pp   £6.99
PB   0 00 719080 8

Yoga
All the tips and techniques you need to get healthy in mind and body

192pp   £8.99
PB   0 00 719091 3

Pilates
All the tips and techniques you need to get a lithe, flexible body

192pp   £8.99
PB   0 00 719063 8

Guitar
All the gear, techniques and tips you need to play the guitar

192pp   £9.99
PB   0 00 719088 3

DIY
All the know-how you need to get doing it yourself

192pp   £8.99
PB   0 00 719447 1

Weddings
All the facts, advice and inspiration you need for the perfect wedding

208pp   £9.99
PB   0 00 719703 9

Drawing & Sketching
All the techniques and inspiration you need to start drawing

192pp   £8.99
PB   0 00 719327 0

Birdwatching
All the tips and techniques you need to get into birdwatching

192pp   £8.99
PB   0 00 719527 3

The World
All the maps and facts you need to know

192pp   £7.99
PB   0 00 719831 0

Dog Training
All the ideas and techniques you need to transform your dog into a well-behaved, sociable companion

192pp   £9.99
PB   0 00 719980 5

Knots
All the tips and equipment you need to know how to tie knots

192pp   £9.99
PB   0 00 719979 1

Kama Sutra
All the ideas and techniques you need to enjoy a fantastic sex life

192pp   £9.99
PB   0 00 719582 9

To order any of these titles, please telephone **0870 787 1732**. For further information about all Collins books, visit our website: **www.collins.co.uk**